Managing intense emotions and overcoming self-destructive habits

The treatment of personality disorder is a major concern facing current mental health services. Specialist therapies are often not available and many people with these problems drop out of treatment. *Managing Intense Emotions and Overcoming Self-Destructive Habits* is a self-help manual for people who would meet the diagnosis of 'emotionally unstable' or 'borderline personality disorder' (BPD), outlining a brief intervention which is based on a model of treatment known to be effective for other conditions, such as anxiety, depression and bulimia.

The manual describes the problem areas, the skills needed to overcome them and how these skills can be developed. It is designed to be used with the help of professional mental health staff, ideally in a group, with individual sessions to support and coach the person in the application of the skills taught. A minimum of 24 and maximum of 36 sessions are recommended. Areas covered include:

- The condition and controversy surrounding diagnosis of BPD
- Drug and alcohol misuse
- Emotional dysregulation and the role of thinking habits and beliefs
- Depression and difficult mood states
- Childhood abuse and relationship difficulties
- Anger management

Borderline personality disorder is a complex and challenging condition. This manual aims to explain the problems experienced by people who may be given this diagnosis in a way that clients and staff can easily understand. It will be essential reading for people with BPD and professionals involved in their care – psychologists, psychiatric nurses, psychiatrists and occupational therapists.

Dr Lorraine Bell is Consultant Clinical Psychologist for Portsmouth HealthCare NHS Trust. She has worked in adult mental health services for 20 years and specialises in the treatment of women with serious mental health problems.

Managing intense emotions and overcoming self-destructive habits

A Self-Help Manual

LORRAINE BELL

Brunner-Routledge
Taylor & Francis Group

HOVE AND NEW YORK

First published 2003 by Brunner-Routledge
27 Church Road, Hove, East Sussex BN3 2FA

Simultaneously published in the USA and Canada
by Brunner-Routledge
29 West 35th Street, New York, NY 10001

Reprinted 2004

Brunner-Routledge is an imprint of the Taylor & Francis Group

Cover design by Sandra Heath
Typeset in Stone Serif by Mayhew Typesetting, Rhayader, Powys
Printed and bound in Great Britain by TJ International, Padstow, Cornwall

British Library Cataloguing in Publication Data
A catalogue record for this book is available from the British Library

Library of Congress Cataloging-in-Publication Data
Bell, Lorraine, 1956–
    Managing intense emotions and overcoming self-destructive habits :
a self-help manual/Lorraine Bell.
        p. cm.
Includes bibliographical references and index.
ISBN 1-58391-915-5 (pbk.)
1. Borderline personality disorder–Treatment–Handbooks, manuals,
etc. I. Title.

RC569.5.B67 B45 2002
616.85'852–dc21

2002071245

ISBN 1-58391-915-5

Contents

Acknowledgements

I would like to thank all those staff and clients who contributed to the pilot of the manual, and Susan Simpson and Dr Fiona Kennedy and other colleagues for their feedback on the original manuscript. Thanks also to Chris Dugan for the cartoons.

I would also like to acknowledge the important contribution of specialists in this field from whom I have learned – in particular Tony Ryle, Marsha Linehan and Jeff Young. Most importantly, I thank all the clients I have known with borderline problems; you have been my teachers.

Lorraine Bell
Consultant Clinical Psychologist
October 2000

PART 1

Understanding the problems and first steps

C H A P T E R 1

Introduction

Who the manual is for and how to use it

This programme is designed to help a particular group of people who suffer with intense emotional states and have a wide range of problems, including extreme mood swings and instability in relationships. These problems are very difficult to manage and often lead to behaviours such as self-harm, drug or alcohol misuse or eating problems. The programme describes these problems and the skills you need to develop to overcome them, and gives instructions for how these skills can be developed. It is designed to be used with the help of professional mental health staff, ideally in a group, with additional individual sessions to support and coach the person in the use of the manual. Thirty-six sessions are recommended for people with borderline personality disorder (BPD), and 24 for people with impulsive or partial borderline problems.

COMMON PROBLEMS

These are the kinds of problems you may experience:

- getting bored easily and doing risky things 'for the hell of it'
- losing your temper a lot
- being moody, getting irritable
- hating the way you look, changing your appearance a lot (hair, clothes, make-up)
- feeling desolate and lonely when alone
- feeling uncomfortable in a close relationship, or that people are trying to control you
- flirting habitually and getting a buzz from sexually attracting others
- feeling very jealous of other people, especially if they are liked by people you want to like you
- being suspicious of people and feeling paranoid (e.g. thinking that people are talking about you)
- having sex with people you don't know well in the hope of getting affection
- getting a buzz from doing things you're not supposed to, like stealing, getting lifts from strangers, taking drugs
- hating or blaming yourself at times and/or hating or blaming others

- doing things to try and please people and get them to like you (e.g. buying them presents)
- neglecting yourself and doing things which are not good for you or harmful
- finding it difficult to maintain relationships
- not knowing who you are and looking for something or someone to give you a sense of identity
- changing life goals, priorities, feelings, or confusion about these
- rapid intense changes in mood
- overwhelming urges to hurt or punish yourself
- not coping when people leave you, desperately clinging on to them or going to extreme lengths to try and get them back
- feeling deeply unloved and longing for someone to take care of you.

One common feature in these problems is instability – instability in one's sense of identity, in mood (highs and lows) and in relationships (idealising someone one minute then devaluing them the next). Another is intense states of emotional pain which are difficult to cope with. Many people with these problems try to numb themselves when in such states, or block them out with alcohol or drugs. They tend to have powerful impulses which in states of distress they find difficult to control. Men and women tend to act on these impulses differently. Men are more likely to use drugs and alcohol and women to develop eating problems (Zanarini *et al.*, 1998).

People with such problems may meet criteria for what is known as *borderline personality disorder* (from now on referred to as BPD) (APA, 1994). This is also called *emotionally unstable personality disorder* (WHO, 1992), which is a more accurate but less well-known term and is not widely used. 'Personality' is made up of your *temperament*, which is biological and genetic, and your *character* which develops out of early experience (Vaillant, 1987). The term 'personality disorder' refers to a wide range of problems which begin in childhood or adolescence, affect many areas of life, tend to last for many years and are not easily changed. Personality problems vary in degree. All of us have aspects of our personality which may be problematic and persistent, though these may be restricted to particular settings. People whose problems would meet criteria for a 'personality disorder' would have more severe problems, and probably in a wider range of settings. There are a number of different personality problems or so-called disorders. BPD is the most common in mental health care because people with borderline problems have acute distress and severe problems in coping. Some people who have intense emotional distress and problematic behaviours like substance misuse and self-harm would not meet the criteria required for a diagnosis of BPD.

Some clinicians would describe people with such problems as 'multi-impulsive'. In this manual the full range of these problems will be referred to as 'borderline problems'.

E X E R C I S E 1.1

At this point it is helpful for you to identify the range of problems you have and how severe they are. Spitzer *et al.* (1987) converted the diagnostic criteria for BPD into a series of questions. The questions below have been revised to include the most recent diagnostic criteria. People do not always realise they have a problem. (What we are used to may seem normal or we may feel the problem is someone else's fault.) It may be helpful to discuss these with someone you trust who knows you well, or with your 'guide'. Circle which of the answers describe you most accurately.

A   Do your relationships with people you really care about have lots of ups and downs? Are there times when you thought they were everything to you and then other times when you thought they were terrible? How many relationships are like this?

1 My feelings toward people in close relationships don't change that much.
2 I do experience different feelings in close relationships, but these are not intense or frequent.
3 I have had one prolonged relationship or several brief relationships in which I have experienced changes in intense positive and negative feelings.

B   Have you often done things impulsively? What kinds of things? Tick if you have done any of the following

	Never	Sometimes	Often
◉ buying things you couldn't afford			
◉ having sex with people you hardly know, or having 'unsafe' sex			
◉ drinking too much			
◉ taking illegal drugs			
◉ driving recklessly			
◉ uncontrollable eating			
◉ shoplifting or stealing			
◉ gambling			

Which is true for you?

1 I am never impulsive.
2 I am impulsive in one area that could be self-damaging.
3 I am impulsive in two or more areas that could be self-damaging.

C   Are you a 'moody' person? How long do your bad moods last? How often do these mood changes happen?

1 My mood does not change much.
2 I am a little moody.
3 I have frequent mood shifts.

D   Do you often have temper outbursts, or get so angry that you lose control? Do you ever hit people, damage property or throw things? Do you ever provoke an argument or get into fights? Do even little things get you very angry?

1 I am rarely angry.
2 I do get angry but it isn't a major problem.
3 I frequently lose my temper, am constantly angry, or have diffi-culty controlling my anger. I tend to get into physical fights.

E   Have you tried to hurt or kill yourself or threatened to do so? Have you ever taken an overdose? Have you ever scratched, cut or burnt yourself or done things like that?

1 I have never harmed myself.
2 I deliberately harmed myself once.
3 I have harmed myself two or more times.

F   Are you different with different people, or in different situ-ations, so that you sometimes do not know who you really are? What examples can you think of? Are you often confused about your long-term goals or career plans? Do you often change your mind about the type of friends or lovers you want? Are you often not sure about what your real values are?

1 My sense of identity is quite stable.
2 My sense of identity is a little unstable.
3 I am often uncertain about at least two of the following: self-image, sexual orientation, long-term goals or career choice, type of friends desired, preferred values.

G   Do you often feel bored or empty inside?

1 I rarely feel bored or empty inside.
2 I sometimes feel bored or empty inside.
3 I often feel bored or empty inside.

H   Have you often become frantic when you thought that some-one you really cared about was going to leave you? What have you done at these times? Did you plead with him or her or try to prevent them from leaving, or try to reject or abandon them first?

1 I cope with separation reasonably well.
2 There was one time when I felt abandoned and this was difficult for me.
3 I hate to feel abandoned and sometimes frantically try to avoid feeling or being abandoned. This has happened at least twice.

If you get a score of three for at least five of the questions then you may meet criteria for what is called *borderline personality disorder* (BPD) or *emotionally unstable personality disorder*. The term 'personality disorder' is associated with negative images. Understandably, you may feel uncomfortable with this 'label'. Because of the stigma of such a diagnosis, and because mental health staff may not understand the condition very well, many people who meet criteria for BPD never receive a formal diagnosis. Whilst labels can feel negative and limiting, there may be advantages to identifying a cluster of problems which tend to persist. Let's examine some of the pros and cons of being given this diagnosis.

PROS AND CONS OF HAVING A DIAGNOSIS

Pros

⊙ Identifying the 'syndrome' acknowledges that the person has real problems rather than being a bad person. It should help both staff and clients understand that it will not be easy for clients to change their behaviour and thinking and, that this will only happen gradually over a long period of time.
⊙ Knowledge and research about the disorder can provide understanding and helpful information. For example, people with borderline problems find it difficult to stay in therapy and do not respond so well to treatments which only focus on one part of the problem (anxiety, depression, eating disorders, etc.).
⊙ There are defined behaviours with this diagnosis. When people change they may no longer meet criteria. This can provide clients and staff with positive feedback.

Cons

⊙ The label 'personality disorder' is stigmatising and may be confused with other severe personality problems, or be seen as an indication of hopelessness about change.

⊙ People may feel you are unlikely to respond to therapy and therefore not refer you to therapists.
⊙ Some staff may not take your problems seriously and dismiss them as exaggerated or 'manipulative'.

Because of the stigma associated with the term BPD it has been suggested that it should be abandoned (Herman, 1992). However, whatever term took its place may become equally stigmatised. It is more important for staff to understand the disorder and those with borderline problems. Many people who work in mental health services now have a more compassionate attitude towards people with personality problems than they would have had in the past. There has also been a shift in attitude about who may benefit from therapy. There is an increased understanding that therapy can be helpful to people with severe mental health problems. Having a personality disorder does not mean you can't change, or that things are hopeless. It means that your difficulties are widespread, affecting many areas of your life, and that change requires persistent effort and determination. This is important for you, for your family, and for those trying to help you, to understand. Just as your early experiences influenced how your personality developed, so can how you live your life, your habits of thought and actions positively change your personality.

ALTERNATIVE TERMS

If you also binge eat or purge (make yourself sick, take laxatives or diuretics or compulsively exercise on a regular basis), and are dissatisfied with your body image, you could describe your problem as 'multi-impulsive bulimia' (Lacey and Evans, 1986).

About a third of people with BPD meet criteria for *post-traumatic stress disorder* or PTSD (Swartz *et al.*, 1990). Some authors such as Herman and colleagues (1986) have argued that BPD could be better described as chronic post-traumatic stress disorder. However, up to one-third of people with BPD do not report abuse or abandonment (Gunderson *et al.*, 1980; Walsh, 1977). *Attention-deficit hyperactivity disorder* (ADHD or ADD) is a condition usually diagnosed in children. Some people question whether it is a valid diagnosis. Adults diagnosed with ADHD and people with BPD may share the following: impulsivity, rapid mood changes, and a low frustration and anger threshold (Wender *et al.*, 1981; Tzelepis *et al.*, 1995). However, ADHD sufferers have problems with inattention and hyperactivity as well as impulsivity. By contrast, people with BPD have more severe problems which have a major impact on their ability to cope with life and relationships.

USING THIS MANUAL

You are likely to have a wide range of problems in different areas of your life. You will be more aware of or unhappy about some of these than about others. They may all need to be addressed, but can't be tackled all at once. This programme tries to help you systematically tackle your problems, one by one. However, the manual is not a substitute for more intensive or comprehensive treatment. If you can get psychotherapy, day treatment, dialectic behaviour therapy or residential treatment in a therapeutic community, these are recommended. With any form of treatment you will need to be very committed to developing your life skills and working at your problems for a long period of time.

In order to benefit from this programme you need to:

⊙ Stay alive!
⊙ Get to sessions drug- and alcohol-free so you can think clearly and remember what is discussed.
⊙ Spend most of your time sober and street drug-free so you can try and manage your problems more constructively. (Homework is the biggest part of the programme.)
⊙ Do the exercises and practise what is suggested. Just turning up or even reading the manual is unlikely to be of much benefit. Research with similar programmes shows that people benefit in proportion to how much of the manual they read and how many of the exercises they carry out.
⊙ Be able to manage any difficult feelings that may surface. If this is likely to be a problem discuss this in your treatment and make a plan together of what coping strategies you will use. Your list should include contact numbers you can use to talk over your feelings or get help, such as the duty mental health services in working hours and 'out of hours' and the Samaritans. Write these on a card and keep this with you (e.g. in your purse or wallet).

If you are attempting suicide regularly, you're only likely to benefit from the programme if you are getting a lot of help, if necessary in a residential setting. If you're using a lot of street drugs and/or alcohol, then you will need to tackle this part of your problem first, perhaps with specialist help from drug and alcohol services. In most parts of the country there's a range of services available depending on your age. They include professional and voluntary sector services such as Alcoholics Anonymous (AA) and Narcotics Anonymous (NA). Thousands of people have benefited from the help of AA or NA. If you want to do the programme, but still have a problem in this area, these organisations may be able to provide you with valuable support.

REFERENCES

American Psychiatric Association (1994). *Diagnostic and Statistical Manual IV*. Washington, DC: APA.

Gunderson, J.G., Kerr, J. and Englund, D.W. (1980). The families of borderlines: a comparative study. *Archives of General Psychiatry*, 132(1), 1–10.

Herman, J. (1992). *Trauma and Recovery*. New York: Basic Books.

Herman, J., Russell, D. and Trocki, K. (1986). Long-term effects of incestuous abuse in childhood. *American Journal of Psychiatry*, 143(10), 1293–1296.

Lacey, J.H. and Evans, C.D.H. (1986). The impulsivist: a multi-impulsive personality disorder. *British Journal of Addiction*, 81, 641–649.

Spitzer, R.L., Williams, J.B. and Gibson, M. (1987) *Structured Clinical Interview for DSM III R Axis II Disorders (SCID II)*. New York: New York State Psychiatric Institute Biometrics Research.

Swartz, M., Blazer, D., George, L. and Winfield, I. (1990). Estimating the prevalence of borderline personality disorder in the community. *Journal of Personality Disorders*, 4(3), 257–272.

Tzelepis, A., Schubiner, H. and Warbasse, L.H. (1995). Differential diagnosis and psychiatric comorbidity patterns in adult attention deficit disorder. In K.G. Nadeau (ed.), *A Comprehensive Guide to Attention Deficit Disorder in Adults: Research, Diagnosis and Treatment* (pp. 35–57). New York: Brunner-Mazel.

Vaillant, G.E. (1987). A developmental view of old and new perspectives of interpersonal behaviours and personality disorders. *Journal of Personality Disorders*, 4, 329–341.

Walsh, F. (1977). Family study 1976: 14 new borderline cases. In R.R. Grinker and B.C. Werble (eds), *The Borderline Patient* (pp. 121–126). New York: Jason Aronson.

Wender, P.H., Reimherr, F.W. and Wood, D.R. (1981). Attention Deficit Disorder ('minimal brain dysfunction') in adults: a replication study of diagnosis and drug treatment. *Archives of General Psychiatry*, 38, 449–456.

World Health Organisation (1992). *International Classification of Diseases – ICD-10*. Washington, DC: World Health Organisation.

Zanarini, M.C., Frankenburg, F.R., Dubo, E.D., Sickel, A.E., Trikha, A., Levin, A. and Reynolds, V. (1998). Axis I co-morbidity of borderline personality disorder. *American Journal of Psychiatry*, 155(12), 1733–1739.

WEBSITES

http://www.psychnet-uk.com/
http://www.soulselfhelp.on.ca/border.html

Review of Chapter 1

Please circle your answer to each of the following:

Are you a Client or 'Guide'?

How much of the chapter did you read?

0%   25%   50%   75%   100%

Overall, was it

Very helpful   Helpful   Don't know   Unhelpful

Did you/your client complete Exercise 1.1?

Yes   No

Was it

Very helpful   Helpful   Don't know   Unhelpful

Comments

Notes for mental health professionals

UNDERSTANDING BORDERLINE PROBLEMS

BPD is relatively rare; that is, the number of people who develop BPD (incidence) is low. However, the number of people with BPD in the community or using psychiatric services at any one point in time (prevalence) is much higher. This is because the condition lasts for many years. (Rates vary between 1.1 per cent and 4.6 per cent in different studies.) People with borderline problems typically have other problems such as depression, anxiety or eating disorders, which are both acute at times and long term. This often leads to high, if intermittent, use of mental health and other health services. However, people with borderline problems rarely respond well to conventional treatment, particularly those geared to single disorders like depression or bulimia nervosa. They can also find it difficult to sustain the commitment to longer-term therapy. For a number of reasons, generic mental health services may fail to help people with borderline problems effectively (Nehls, 1998). For example, clients can fall between mental health and substance misuse services, with either service declining to help them because of their 'other' problems. Such responses by services can repeat or perpetuate cycles of rejection or neglect that clients have experienced in their family life or childhood.

Psychiatric diagnostic manuals list a number of problematic behaviours but do not attempt to formulate or understand the nature and origin of these problems. The *Diagnostic and Statistical Manual* (APA, 1994) gives the following description of BPD:

Individuals with BPD make frantic efforts to avoid real or imagined abandonment (Criterion 1).
The perception of impending separation or rejection, or the loss of external structure, can lead to profound changes in self-image, affect, cognition and behavior. These individuals are very sensitive to environmental circumstances. They experience intense abandonment fears and inappropriate anger even when faced with a realistic time-limited separation, or when there are unavoidable changes in plans (e.g. sudden despair in reaction to a clinician announcing the end of the hour; panic or fury when someone important to them is just a few minutes late or must cancel an appointment). They may believe that this

'abandonment' implies they need to have other people with them. Their frantic efforts to avoid abandonment may include impulsive actions such as self-mutilating or suicidal behaviours, which are described separately in criterion 5.

Individuals with BPD have a pattern of unstable and intense relationships (Criterion 2).
They may idealise potential caregivers or lovers at the first or second meeting, demand to spend a lot of time together, and share the most intimate details early in a relationship. However, they may switch quickly from idealising other people to devaluing them, feeling that the other person does not care enough, does not give them enough, is not 'there' enough. These individuals can empathise with and nurture other people, but only with the expectation that the other person will 'be there' in return to meet their own needs on demand. These individuals are prone to sudden and dramatic shifts in their view of others, who may alternately be seen as beneficent supports or as cruelly punitive. Such shifts often reflect disillusionment with a caregiver whose nurturing qualities had been idealised or whose rejection or abandonment is expected.

There may be an identity disturbance characterised by markedly and persistently unstable self-image or sense of self (Criterion 3).
There are sudden and dramatic shifts in self-image, characterised by shifting goals, values and vocational aspirations. There may be sudden changes in opinions and plans about career, sexual identity, values and type of friends . . . Although they usually have a self-image that is based on being bad or evil, individuals with this disorder may at times have feelings that they do not exist at all. Such experiences usually occur in situations in which the individual feels a lack of a meaningful relationship, nurturing and support. These individuals may show worse performance in unstructured work or school situations.

Individuals with this disorder display impulsivity in at least two areas that are potentially self-damaging (Criterion 4).
They may gamble, spend money irresponsibly, binge eat, misuse substances, engage in unsafe sex, or drive recklessly.

Individuals with BPD display recurrent suicidal behaviour, gestures or threats or self-mutilating behaviour (Criterion 5).
Completed suicide occurs in 8–10% of such individuals and self-mutilative acts (e.g. cutting, burning) and suicide threats and attempts are very common. Recurrent suicidality is often the reason that these individuals present for help. These self-destructive acts are usually precipitated by threats of separation or rejection or by expectation that they assume increased responsibility. Self-mutilation may occur during dissociative experiences and often brings relief by reaffirming the ability to feel or by expiating the individual's sense of being evil.

Individuals with BPD may display affective instability that is due to a marked reactivity of mood (e.g. intense episodic dysphoria, irritability, or anxiety usually lasting a few hours and only rarely more than a few days) (Criterion 6).
The basic dysphoric mood of those with BPD is often disrupted by periods of anger, panic or despair and is rarely relieved by periods of well-being or satisfaction. These episodes may reflect the individual's extreme reactivity to interpersonal stresses.

Individuals with BPD may be troubled by chronic feelings of emptiness (Criterion 7).
Easily bored, they may constantly seek something to do.

Individuals with BPD frequently express inappropriate intense anger or have difficulty controlling their anger (Criterion 8).
They may display extreme sarcasm, enduring bitterness or verbal outbursts. The anger is often elicited when a caregiver or lover is seen as neglectful, withholding, uncaring or abandoning. Such expressions of anger are often followed by shame and guilt and contribute to the feeling they have of being evil.

During periods of extreme stress, transient paranoid ideation or dissociative symptoms (e.g. depersonalisation) may occur (Criterion 9)
These are generally of insufficient severity or duration to warrant an additional diagnosis. These episodes occur most frequently in response to real or imagined abandonment. Symptoms tend to be transient, lasting minutes or hours. The real or perceived return of the caregiver's nurturance may result in a remission of symptoms.

APA (1994) describes BPD as one type of *emotionally unstable personality disorder*, a term which is more readily understood by clients and less likely to invoke negative attitudes by staff. The other subtype of 'emotionally unstable personality disorder' is described as 'impulsive' (i.e. more likely to take out anger on others). There is no empirical basis for this distinction, though men may be more likely to become 'impulsive', while women 'borderline'.

WORKING WITH PEOPLE WITH BORDERLINE PROBLEMS

A number of studies identify negative attitudes and responses to people with BPD by hospital nursing and medical staff (Fraser and Gallop, 1993; Gallop and Wynn, 1987; Gallop *et al.*, 1989). Miller and Davenport (1996) demonstrated that staff knowledge and attitudes could be improved with a self-paced instructional programme. People with borderline problems are often disliked by staff. They may be seen as demanding care – overtly (e.g. screaming to be helped or stating that no one cares) or covertly (perhaps showing their anguish through self-harm), but not getting better! This attitude may partly stem from a failure to understand the degree of desperation and genuine lack of coping skills when in such states. Clients may deliberately try to gain the attention and concern of staff at times, but this needs to be understood in the context of the person's experience and limited repertoire for coping and/or help-seeking. Staff also tend to overestimate the ability of these clients to cope, and feel their need or demand for immediate help is unreasonable and exaggerated. Most people with borderline problems have a genuine need for care as they have often had very deprived or abusive backgrounds. They also have limited access to care as adults (Nehls, 1999).

Staff may behave in ways which replicate the invalidation, neglect, rejection, and even abuse that clients have experienced from early caretakers. People with borderline problems can also fill this role, usually towards themselves or at times towards others. The latter is particularly likely in men with borderline problems whose conditioning as males increases the likelihood for them to take out their rage on others. Clients may also have more subtle ways of behaving self-destructively, e.g. by sabotaging relationships. It is very important that staff do not get recruited by the client into rejection even when the client may go to dramatic lengths to test them out or 'invite' rejection!

People with borderline problems are interesting people who can be very rewarding to work with, especially when we are able to work with them long enough to see them make progress. There are a number of ways people with borderline problems can be challenging to work with:

- Finding it difficult to trust us. This can lead to them not disclosing important things or being silent in the session.
- Making intense attachments to us and feeling unable to cope without us. We can have different reactions to this – we may reciprocate this special role and feel we are the only person who can help the client. Alternatively, we may avoid this by distancing ourselves, or by being too directive or intellectual with clients.
- Being provocative and challenging boundaries.
- Getting angry with us or describing incidents in which they have been violent to others without acknowledging their responsibility for this. Impulsive or unmanageable anger is not a problem for all clients with borderline problems. (Those who do not enact anger may have similarly powerful feelings of anger which are hidden, suppressed or directed towards themselves.)
- Being very sensitive to experiences of feeling controlled. This can contribute to people not complying with requests or acting defiantly. This includes not sitting down in sessions, not looking at us, arriving late, dropping out of therapy to avoid us having control over when therapy ends.
- Making considerable emotional demands; for example, asking us direct personal questions and saying challenging things like 'You don't like me do you?' Clients with borderline problems often notice when staff aren't authentic and can get on better with untrained staff who are more natural with them.
- Needing help at times that are less convenient to the service (i.e. late evenings and weekends) and needing help urgently.

If a client contacts us when they are acutely distressed this is usually a very positive and risky step for them as it probably means they are trusting us. Working with clients with borderline problems involves a willingness to be open and flexible and engage with them at very painful times. Whilst certain boundaries are very important (e.g. never to have sexual contact with clients), other boundaries need to be more flexible. In particular, clients should be encouraged to contact the service out of hours to help prevent self-harm (see pp. 20–21).

Skills and qualities needed, and key tasks involved when helping people with borderline problems, are:

- compassion, patience and empathy;
- identifying risk and working with a hierarchy of priority (preserving life first then tackling 'treatment-interfering behaviours');
- building and maintaining a therapeutic alliance, monitoring and dealing constructively with disruptions to the therapeutic relationship;
- agreeing, keeping to and maintaining boundaries;
- educating patients about borderline problems and problem-solving, and working collaboratively and encouraging people to find their own solutions to problems;
- encouraging people to manage their relationships assertively and honestly, both in their daily life and within the health service;
- helping the client to access community resources and other services;
- dealing with challenging behaviour – respecting the client; acknowledging their feelings and firmly stating a request for appropriate behaviour and, if necessary, setting limits.

THE PROGRAMME

The programme is designed for people with borderline problems to use with training, supervision and support from professional mental health staff. It is not the recommended treatment for BPD but provides a structured therapeutic programme where specialist treatments (dialectic behaviour therapy, intensive psychodynamic day care or residential treatment in a therapeutic community) are unavailable.

The most successful format for this programme is likely to be a skills training group led by a psychologist or cognitive behaviour therapist (ideally with two facilitators) and concurrent individual support sessions by another experienced mental health professional who has some training in CBT. The pilot study of the programme found that clients needed both structured skills training and regular time to talk over their problems and how to implement the skills in their own daily life. Ideally clients will have additional weekly appointments for a minimum of 30 minutes for the duration of the group. People with BPD have numerous crises and will also benefit from access to out-of-hours support services, medical assessment and treatment by a senior psychiatrist and a key worker or care co-ordinator (see pp. 21–22).

The manual is designed to be presented in 24–36 weekly sessions of 1–2 hours. The number and duration of sessions will depend on the size of the group and the severity of their problems. Multi-impulsive clients, or those who are stable and unlikely to be hospitalised, could receive 24 sessions as outlined below. If clients are attempting suicide and likely to be hospitalised 36 sessions are probably needed. This could be carried out over three phases of 12 sessions which can be planned around staff and public holidays, for example beginning September/October, January and April/May. This builds in breaks for staff and clients, enabling both to make a consistent commitment to deliver or attend the sessions. It also mirrors a typical education timetable, which is an appropriate model for clients. If possible, certificates should be presented to those who complete. Running the skills training group is not recommended unless you are confident and skilled in running groups *and* working with this client group.

Planning the programme well in advance and having a clear contract is important, so that all parties are clear about what is expected of them. Clients need to understand that the programme involves commitment on their part and that what they get out will be proportional to what they put in. The timetable is very tight. This needs to be emphasised so that clients try their utmost not to miss sessions.

Effective participation in the programme requires that all parties

- Can read!
- Have some motivation to understand and explore the client's problems and consider alternative ways of dealing with them.
- Are willing to commit to the programme and systematically tackle the client's problems. This needs the client to be alert and sober enough for these meetings and at other times to practise new coping strategies.

The programme is not suitable, or should be suspended, if a client's substance misuse or propensity for violence is so severe that they cannot effectively participate. The programme is designed for people in the community but could be used in a medium- or long-term residential setting. In such a setting the skills training could be provided more frequently than once per week, but an open format (new members joining at intervals) is likely to be confusing for clients and staff and is not recommended.

If a client misses four consecutive sessions without giving a reason they are usually withdrawn from the programme. This should be explained at the outset. If clients have so many crises that they can't use the programme in a systematic way, then they may need extra support or not be ready for this programme. If clients are withdrawn it should be explained that they may be able to use such an intervention in the future, and the conditions needed for them to do so successfully explained.

If possible, give clients one chapter at a time as you work through it. I would suggest clients read all but one chapter as they may not have realised they had a problem in that area or have felt able to disclose it. The exception to this is Chapter 10, which is for people who deliberately self-harm. When you reach the section in the programme which addresses child abuse check then whether this is a problem for them or not. If you are both clear that they have not experienced significant abuse or neglect they can miss those sessions. (There is a high correlation between abuse and self-harm, but this cannot be assumed in every case.) At each group session:

⊙ ask clients to share something they are pleased with from the last week, and encourage them to validate themselves and learn to select positive information;
⊙ review their home study;
⊙ once mindfulness is taught, finish with 5 minutes mindfulness of breathing or variation.

Once this is established you can invite members to suggest variations – for example, mindfulness at the start of the meeting and something they are proud of at the end.

SUGGESTED SESSION PLAN FOR PART I[1]

Session 1. Introductions. Give Chapter 1. Outline programme – client reads each chapter and completes exercises between sessions. These are then discussed the following session. Agree timetable and ground rules. Discuss areas covered in manual. Clients may need to keep other issues 'in reserve' to review at a later date. Discuss Exercise 1.1 and diagnosis.

---

[1] Notes are not given for Part II as this will vary according to the needs of particular clients.

Session 2. Give out, and look at, Chapter 3. Do family tree and discuss. What parts of their family history is relevant to their problems? Home study – ask client to try life line or life story and complete review. Discuss if they are likely to find it challenging and, if so, how they will manage.

Session 3. Discuss homework. What have they learnt? Give out Chapter 4. Discuss and complete checklists. Home study – food and exercise diary. Ask client to complete all checklists and review of Chapter 3.

Session 4. Review diaries and discuss reflectively. Complete Chapter 4. Would they like to set any goals? Give out Chapter 5. Home study – read Chapter 5 and complete review of Chapter 4. Also ask clients to keep drug and alcohol diary (exercise 5.1, p. 56). Check client understands diary and reinforce importance of this.

Session 5. Look at drug and alcohol use (diary from Chapter 5) and discuss what it gives them. Do they have any concerns? Discuss possible consequences. Would they like to set any goals (don't push)? Give out Chapter 6, ask client to review Chapter 5 and do first half of Chapter 6, including Exercise 6.1 (identifying difficult emotional states).

Session 6. Look at Exercise 6.1 (p. 65). Explain importance of recognising these emotional states and when they are in them. Ask group to identify how they know when they are in each state. Do Exercise 6.3. Are there times when they handle these states better than others? Need to problem-solve here. Introduce the idea of a behavioural experiment and invite people to set a small goal for this week. Ask clients to finish Chapter 6 and complete emotions diary (see p. 66) and Exercise 6.3.

Session 7. Discuss skilful means and practise mindfulness skills. Discuss the middle way and do Exercise 6.8. Home study – practise mindfulness and complete other exercises in Chapter 6.

Session 8. Did they try mindfulness exercises and how did they get on? Complete Chapter 6. Discuss if they need a cue card for crises. Give out Chapter 7. Home study – read up to p. 82 and practise mindfulness.

Session 9. Do they understand the role of thoughts and beliefs? Discuss Exercises 7.1, 7.2 and 7.3 (pp. 81, 85, 86). Ask them to read the rest of Chapter 7 and keep a thought diary all week.

Session 10. Discuss how they successfully challenge negative thinking. Introduce schemas. Home study – complete Schema questionnaire and do Exercise 7.4 (diary).

Session 11. Ask each client to give an example of how they challenged a negative thought. Score Schema questionnaire and complete grid. Identify and discuss key schema. Home study – Exercise 7.7. Remind the client that at the next session you decide which of the remaining chapters in Part II to prioritise.

Session 12. Clarify schema maintenance, avoidance and compensation. Review evidence for one schema. Ask client to complete review for Chapter 7 and give out Chapter 8. Ask client to complete Parenting questionnaire. Agree how to allocate the remaining sessions from the options in Part II. (You can give out all chapters except Chapter 10, which should only be given out if the client does self-harm.)

Sessions 13–36. Complete Part II as negotiated with client.

ADDITIONAL SUPPORT

Clients will need individual sessions in addition to the skills training group. These are usually weekly for 30 minutes, are scheduled at a regular time, and have a twofold purpose: first, to give more time for the client to discuss applying the skills taught within the programme in her daily life; second, to have time to air and process crises. The latter should be related to problem-solving and coping skills taught in the programme. If sessions are missed or cancelled with short notice you need to discuss why.

People with borderline problems need high levels of support, and mental health services can fail to appreciate the extent of their genuine needs and potential to benefit from treatment. This can contribute to clients feeling they may only get professional time if they show how desperate they feel by harming themselves or threatening to harm themselves. (Unfortunately, this rarely has the desired effect as staff may then blame clients for being 'manipulative'.) Many people with borderline problems have not had the care they needed and so may not trust that care will be there for them without dramatising their need and anguish. Experiences in psychiatric units, especially residential units, can often repeat these experiences of neglect and reinforce the factors that may contribute to repetitive self-harm.

Those difficult times when your client feels they cannot cope are windows of opportunity for them to try something different and potentially expand their confidence and coping repertoire. You will have the maximum potential in helping them learn these skills if you can help them problem-solve whilst they are in the middle of the crisis. If you have talked through coping strategies with them, this is a time to remind them of these and help them take the next step towards coping more constructively. This is why dialectic behaviour therapists give clients a phone number to contact them on between sessions when they are in crisis. Generic community services are unlikely to be able to provide this, but you can encourage your client to phone you within working hours. If you cannot return their call, or if it is out of hours, your client may be able to use the duty or out-of-hour services. You will need to discuss with your client when it is appropriate to phone. Clients are encouraged to phone if they have an urge to self-harm but don't feel able to use alternative coping strategies. DBT therapists have a rule that once a client has self-harmed they should not phone for 24 hours. This is to minimise any risk of reinforcement. You need to explain to clients that the main aim of a phone call is to prevent the client from self-harming.

SHARED CARE BY A MULTI-DISCIPLINARY TEAM

Assessment by a senior psychiatrist is recommended for all clients with BPD. Most clients with BPD will need to be under the medical care of a consultant psychiatrist, particularly in the early and acute stages of the disorder. Clients may benefit from medication, in particular mood stabilisers. Toxic drugs (especially tricyclics) should always be avoided and the risk of the accumulation or abuse of medication borne in mind. Clients are very likely to need to use 'duty', 'out-of-hours' or emergency psychiatric services and many people require admissions to psychiatric hospital, whenever possible on a voluntary basis. The benefit of admissions is controversial. Some experts say it should be avoided whenever possible. Certainly clients can learn unhelpful habits in hospital and their problem behaviours can worsen. However, at times of psychosis or continuous risk of suicide, hospital admissions may be necessary.

People with borderline problems who voluntarily access psychiatric services are those who suffer most with mood problems and depression. Other clients (those actively abusing substances or those more aggressive to others) may come to the attention of the services but not engage in them. Those who do engage are likely to need to use the service either intermittently or continuously for many years. Psychological therapy remains the core intervention for people with borderline problems. However, it is important for clients to feel that their local mental health team is approachable in times of need and that their care does not depend on one heroic person! Such a person may fall from favour, feel de-skilled or burnt out, or leave their post. The care of someone with such a complex, long-standing condition should not be left to one individual of any profession.

Those who do not engage in or complete the programme but continue to have major problems will benefit from the long-term support of a community psychiatric nurse or from more intensive treatment such as that provided by tertiary units.

GENERALISATION ACROSS SETTINGS

This is a behavioural concept which is an important part of any learning programme or skills training. For example, if you teach a client to relax they will need to gradually apply this at times when they are anxious. Clients with borderline problems need a lot of coaching in generalising what you cover in a session to times when they are emotionally 'hyped up'. There are a number of ways this can be achieved – for example, a written cue card with coping statements or possible strategies; instructional tapes they can play back in your voice or theirs; crisis phone lines. You may like to consider taping sessions which can be very helpful. All clients should have a personal strategy list for managing a crisis, including a range of numbers they can phone (they will not always get a reply). This can include professional and voluntary services and possibly friends or family. Families and friends can be coached in this role and the crisis line may be extended to them. Clients tend either to go to one person all the time (who is likely to find this burdensome and ultimately reach the limits of their tolerance), or they do not seek help at all for fear of rejection (this is what is called 'schema avoidance'; see Chapter 7). Any one approach may not be or feel successful and clients need to understand that they cannot guarantee 100 per cent helpful responses 100 per cent of the time.

SUPERVISION

In order for you to help your client effectively, all those involved in delivering the programme will need to meet regularly for supervision. Part of the role of supervision is for you to receive an 'injection' of what your client will need from you – a sense of confidence and direction in tackling multiple challenges, motivation, validation of your skills and what you are doing well, clarification of problems and consideration of possible solutions. Linehan emphasises that it is important for staff, like clients, to recognise that we make mistakes (all therapists, like all human beings, are fallible). Part of the supervision contract made by DBT therapists is to search for empathic explanations of each client's behaviour.

THERAPY-INTERFERING BEHAVIOUR

Too often supervision only looks at how clients' behaviour interferes with therapy. All staff and all clients can be seen as having 'therapy interfering behaviours'. Allen (1997) provides a very useful summary of strategies for dealing with how clients can sabotage or 'interfere' with therapy. Can you think of any way *your* responses or behaviour (things you may say or do) could interfere with or obstruct therapy or your relationship with your client? Do you ever find yourself lecturing clients? What do you do when you get impatient or angry with your client? What effect does that have on your client? It is important for you to be open about this with your client in order not to invalidate their experience and to model processing conflict in relationships. Recognising when our behaviour is interfering with or impeding the relationship or work with a client is a central skill in helping people with borderline problems. Ideally we can discuss it in supervision.

TEN CORE REQUIRED SKILLS

Assessment of risk

Many, though not all, clients will have a history of suicide attempts. This does not mean that another attempted suicide will not be fatal. When clients are at risk of attempting suicide they may need more support or protection.

Openness

It is very important that clients have a say in what happens so that they feel an active participant in therapy, that they understand what is going to happen, what you are doing and why. Most people with borderline problems have been abused or have felt very controlled by authority or parental figures. Your relationship needs to be qualitatively different, though at times it will inevitably feel similar for your client. You will need to be aware when this may be happening and encourage your client to talk openly about it. This is something they may not have been encouraged to do, allowed to do, or have felt safe to do in the past.

Boundary setting

Most clients with borderline problems have difficulty understanding the need for setting and keeping boundaries. Some may challenge boundaries. You should as far as possible spell out plainly what boundaries you expect your client to keep in terms of attendance, time-keeping and the purpose and content of the sessions. Other boundaries may need to be explained as they arise (e.g. if the client asks for personal information about you). This should not include interpretations, but enquiries about what the client feels or needs may be helpful. For example, if you are taking annual leave and a client asks where you are going it is quite acceptable to say so. However, if they ask who you are going with, it may be more appropriate to enquire what concerns the client has about that issue. Discussion on such topics should be kept brief and within the frameworks used in the manual. For example, you can identify the client's fear of others being more important as part of a 'fear of abandonment' or 'worthlessness' schema.

Staying warm and keeping your cool

I have never known anyone with borderline problems who has experienced consistently supportive care within relationships. It is important that anyone working with clients with these life experiences does *not*:

⊙ replicate the negative behaviours of other care figures in their lives;
⊙ act out their anger inappropriately;
⊙ have inappropriate expectations of them then get impatient or critical when they don't meet their expectations;
⊙ make promises they don't or can't keep.

When you feel angry or frustrated with a client, you need to look at what both of you may have contributed to that. Allen (1997, 32) warns that therapists should be very careful not to attribute responsibility for interpersonal problems within the therapy entirely to the patient. What patterns can you notice in yourself? Which kind of patients do you find most difficult to work with? Do you know why? It's likely these clients will 'push' any 'buttons' you have. It is important to be aware if you feel you want to parent or look after someone in a way that may reinforce them in a child role rather than an adult role. Some of us in mental health care need people who are dependent on us to play out a role; perhaps one we learnt early in our lives with a needy parent for example. If you need to feel competent you are likely to feel incompetent. If you have a tendency to lose your patience and blame the victim you are likely to do this. Like our clients, we need to steer a 'middle way' between rescuing and rejecting, and to monitor subtle and less subtle patterns of how we respond and relate to people. We need heart and brain in gear at all times. A tall order! Not for the faint-hearted!

Patients may behave in ways which provoke us until we feel angry, unappreciated, attacked, disempowered. This may be the patient's way of getting us to feel what they feel (this is known as projective identification). It helps to be aware what form this is likely to take for each client (abandoned, rejected, humiliated, etc.). How do they commonly experience others? How have they sabotaged relationships in the past?

Cognitive analytic therapy has some very useful tools for mapping these patterns (see Dunn and Parry, 1997). This can be helpful in ensuring that the mental health service does not replicate abusive or rejecting experiences, as can happen, sometimes in part (but only in part), because clients' behaviour provokes it.

Kreisman and Straus (1989) recommend a communication formulae at difficult times with clients (e.g. during confrontations and crises) known as SET; this stands for 'support, empathy and truth'. Communication to the client should attempt to *include all three elements*, though not all may be heard. Support statements assert your commitment to the client and wish to help (this reassures the client about your intent and reminds them of the therapeutic relationship). Empathy statements are like validation (see pp. 28–29) – for example, telling the person you are aware of their pain ('you must be hurting very badly'). Truth statements would include statements like 'no one is going to be hurt' and 'I must ask you to leave', or may address your hypothesis about the client's pattern of behaviour such as 'I think you are trying to get me to reject you. Is that what you really want?' Truth statements need to be said non-judgementally and without anger. SET statements can be helpful to practise in supervision.

Motivational interviewing (MI)

A lot of what your client does you would like them not to! However, there are many reasons why they may not be able or ready to change. There is evidence with other client groups that staff who take a more confrontational approach have higher drop-out rates and poorer outcome. Research demonstrates that the interaction between therapist and client powerfully influences client resistance, compliance and change. Motivational interviewing (Miller and Rollnick, 1991; Miller, 1998) is a directive, client-centred counselling approach which enables clients to explore their ambivalence about change. Its aim is to enhance internal motivation rather than impose change externally. Problems such as denial and resistance are not seen as only characteristics of the client but the outcome of interactions between the client and staff and family relating to them.

Principles of MI include:

- expressing empathy;
- developing discrepancy between 'where I see myself now' and 'where I would like to be';
- *not* arguing, but rolling with resistance;
- *a can do* approach supporting self-efficacy – impart belief in the possibility of change; emphasise choice;
- working collaboratively – starting with the clients' concerns not the guide's.

Strategies include:

- open questions: 'Tell me about . . .'; affirmation: 'It's natural you should have mixed feelings'; effective listening and summarising: 'Is this what you mean? Have I got it right? . . . it sounds like . . .';
- questions and strategies to invoke and aid self-reflection;
- motivational statements – problem recognition; concerns about the effects (now and in the future) on family, friends, health; intention to change; optimism and past experience of self-efficacy;
- evoking motivational statements: for example, 'Do you have any concerns?' 'Have you begun to make any changes?' Don't ask too many questions!
- exploration of concerns, looking back and forward: 'What were your hopes and goals?' 'How does the future seem with or without the problem?'
- exploring goals: 'What is the most important thing in your life?' 'How does your problem get in the way?'
- decisional balance: costs/benefits of change versus costs/benefits of status quo (see Chapter 5).

Don't argue, lecture or persuade with logic; give expert advice at the beginning; order, direct, warn or threaten; do most of the talking; make moral statements; criticise, preach or judge; ask three or more questions in a row; tell the client they have a problem; prescribe solutions.

When your client seems resistant you need to change your strategy! Ways of dealing with resistance include reflecting back ('On the one hand you feel . . ., on the other'), shifting focus, agreeing with a twist ('Yes, but . . .'), emphasising personal choice and control and reframing. You need to avoid the common reactions of confrontation ('Why don't you . . .'), persuasion ('You really should cut down'), blaming the client, expecting

change before the client is ready, coming across as the expert ('This is really bad for you because . . .').

Validation

Linehan has identified both the role of constant invalidation in the development of BPD and the importance of validation as a skill in helping people with borderline problems. Terms like manipulative are rarely appropriate. They should never be used with clients, and if you feel a client is trying to manipulate you or others you need to discuss this with them (and in supervision), considering with your client:

⊙ what their needs are;
⊙ what they want to happen;
⊙ what effect they think their actions/statements will have.

Times when it will be helpful to validate clients include when they have not carried out an agreed task and may expect to be criticised (e.g. by acknowledging that change may be difficult for them). It is especially important to validate clients when they are feeling bad about themselves or ashamed. Any of these are likely when a client self-harms. How can you validate self-destructive behaviour, you may be thinking? You can communicate to your client that you understand that self-harm is an effective way of regulating their emotions (assuming that you do understand how it does; if not, discuss it in supervision). It is important that you validate the valid not the invalid. For example, when someone is 'paranoid' you would not validate their beliefs or assumptions as accurate, rather you would communicate the understanding that you knew they are afraid. You could the hypothesise what they may be afraid of – criticism, feeling rejected, humiliated or betrayed.

Being simultaneously problem- and solution-focused

In order for you or your client not to be overwhelmed by multiple problems, you will need to focus on one problem at a time. This needs to be done in a way that is sensitive to your client's current concerns. You will need to help your client become clear about what the problem is. For example, if they feel lonely and abandoned, is it that they have few friends; if so, what needs to change? Do they need to meet more people or to change the kind of people they mix with or how they behave in relationships? Or do they have friends but not feel cared for (and need to change their beliefs or schemas)? Of course, for many clients all of this is true, which is why they need a lot of help and why a range of approaches may be helpful. You will need an ability to explore and clarify problems, identify their triggers and consequences, and be skilful in highlighting and expanding on each client's potential for finding solutions. It is always helpful to ask 'Are there any times this is not a problem? What was different then? Can you think of any time you felt this way and coped differently? I understand that you feel completely unable to cope when this happens but you know everyone has times when for some reason it isn't quite so bad or we manage to do something differently. Can you remember any other times when you felt awful but didn't get drunk or hurt yourself?'

It's a good rule of thumb to get clients to identify their strengths and alternative coping strategies; rather than have to suggest them – though if necessary do the latter. You may need to be a bit canny about this so as to avoid triggering resistance from feeling controlled. ('I can think of something else you could do but I'm not sure you're ready yet . . .')

Collaborative problem-solving

You will often need to brainstorm with your client creative solutions to their problems and how they manage problematic emotional states. It is very important that you try to help your client find their own solutions rather than tell them what you think they should do. Socratic questioning is a key tool. This was summarised once as 'You know. You tell me', rather than 'I know. I'll tell you'. You can ask them to think about all the different things they could have done and the possible consequences of each. It is also important to remember that people's coping varies and to recognise that there have been times they have coped better. What did they do then? How might others handle the problem differently or more effectively? Layden *et al.* (1993) suggest turning rhetorical questions into literal questions. So if a client says 'What is the point in going on?' ask them 'That's an interesting question . . . what is the point in going on?' If they say 'What am I going to do?' ask 'What *are* you going to do?'

Nehls (2000) gives suggestions for working collaboratively as a case worker.

Dealing with self-harm

One area where staff often struggle to understand, or make assumptions which may be false, is when someone self-harms. Many staff believe that the person's primary motive in harming themselves is to get some kind of response from others. Whilst this can become a factor in a pattern of self-harming, it is rarely the initial motive or main function. People self-harm predominantly in an attempt to regulate intense negative affect or dysphoria (tension, anger or overwhelming sadness). This is a level of distress or anguish which is intense and unbearable, beyond what most of us can imagine. Even where there are consequences (e.g. receipt of physical nursing), these may not be relevant to the maintenance of the behaviour. The best approach is to try to make an individual analysis of the problem with your client. You can explore the problem together, discussing its history (Leibenluft *et al.*, 1987). You can also get your client to record their feelings when they have the urge to self-harm. It is helpful to identify what triggers the self-harm (antecedents), what exactly the person does (behaviour) and what they experience afterwards (consequences). Possible consequences are release of tension, physiological arousal, and converting invisible to visible pain which may or may not be shared with others. It is important to try to enable clients to identify and distinguish between different feelings. For example, anger or fear may trigger in a client the urge to harm themselves, whilst shame or despair may trigger the urge to kill themselves.

Wanting a reaction from others is only one possible function of self-harm. Many people self-harm in private. You are less likely to know about this than if people show you what they have done, so staff often get a distorted understanding about why people self-harm. A useful guide for how to be with a client in acute distress or crisis is to think of how you would ideally be with someone who is hurt and confused. You would listen to what they were distressed about, comfort and reassure them. To be there for them you have to stay calm and, if appropriate, help them calm down by getting them to think of ways of managing their feelings more effectively. When they are calm enough to examine the problem you can look at all the possible ways they can tackle it. For example, how has the client managed better on other occasions with similar feelings, or how would someone else they know try to cope? Wherever possible you need to help your client find their own solutions and thereby learn to take care of themselves. This is better than them relying on you or others, or feeling helpless and incapable of looking after themselves. Self-harming behaviour isn't so 'crazy' when you consider the widespread habits through which many people harm themselves (smoking, heavy drinking, etc.).

Cognitive reappraisal

People with borderline problems have very entrenched patterns of thinking; for example, in all or nothing ways ('Either you are there for me whenever I need you or you don't care about me at all'). Helping clients re-evaluate and modify these thought patterns is a crucial skill. There are a number of techniques and strategies you can use. The book by Layden *et al.* (1993) and the chapter by Beck *et al.* (1990) are particularly helpful. One technique described is that of *continua rating*. You ask a client to rate how bad something is using a scale of 0–100. For example, when they say something minor is a total disaster get them to rate other things (real disasters), then discuss how their ratings are incongruous. When doing this you have to be very careful that you are always respectful as people can feel belittled. Those with borderline problems can be especially prone to feeling you are humiliating or ridiculing them.

FURTHER TRAINING

Training in dialectic behaviour therapy and cognitive analytic therapy is available in the UK, but at the time of publication there is no formal training in schema-focused cognitive therapy outside the USA.

REFERENCES AND SUGGESTED READING

Allen, D.M. (1997). Techniques for reducing therapy-interfering behaviour in patients with borderline personality disorder. *Journal of Psychotherapy Practice and Research*, 6(1), 25–35.

American Psychiatric Association (1994). *Diagnostic and Statistical Manual IV*. Washington, DC: American Psychiatric Association.

Arnold, L. and Magill, A. (1997). *Working with Self-injury A Practical Guide*. Colston Street, Basement Project (UK). (ISBN 1 901335 003).

Beck, A.T. and Freeman, A. *et al.* (1990). Borderline personality disorder. In *Cognitive Therapy of Personality Disorders* (pp. 176–207). London: Guilford Press.

Dunn, M. and Parry, G. (1997). A formulated care plan approach to caring for people with borderline personality disorder in a community mental health service setting. *Clinical Psychology Forum*, 104, 19–22.

Fraser, K. and Gallop, R. (1993). Nurses confirming/disconfirming responses to patients diagnosed with borderline personality disorder. *Archives of Psychiatric Nursing*, 7, 336–341.

Gallop, R., Lancee, W.J. and Garfinkle, P. (1989). How nursing staff respond to the label 'borderline personality disorder'. *Hospital and Community Psychiatry*, 40, 815–819.

Gallop, R. and Wynn, O.F. (1987). The difficult inpatient: identification and response by staff. *Canadian Journal of Psychiatry*, 33, 211–215.

Kreisman, J.J. and Straus, H. (1989). *I Hate You – Don't Leave Me. Understanding the Borderline Personality*. New York: Avon Books.

Langley, M.H. (1993). *Self-management Therapy for Borderline Personality Disorder*. New York: Springer Pub Co.

Layden, M.A., Newman, C.F., Freeman, A. and Byers Morse, S. (1993). *Cognitive Therapy of Borderline Personality Disorder*. Boston, Mass.: Allyn & Bacon.

Leibenluft, E., Gardner, D.L. and Cowdry, R.W. (1987). The inner experience of the borderline self-mutilator. *Journal of Personality Disorders*, 1(4), 317–324.

Linehan, M.M. (1993). *Skills Training Manual for Treating Borderline Personality Disorder*. New York: Guilford Press.

Miller, S.A. and Davenport, N.C. (1996). Increasing staff knowledge of and improving attitudes toward patients with borderline personality disorder. *Psychiatric Services*, 47(5), 533–535.

Miller W.R. (1998). Enhancing motivation for change. In W.R. Miller and N. Heather (eds), *Treating Addictive Behaviours*. New York: Plenum Press.

Miller, W.R. and Rollnick, S. (1991). *Motivational Interviewing: Preparing People to Change Addictive Behaviour*. London: Guilford Press.

Nehls, N. (1998). Borderline personality disorder: gender stereotypes, stigma and limited system of care. *Issues in Mental Health Nursing*, 19(2), 97–112.

Nehls, N. (1999). Borderline personality disorder: the voice of patients. *Res Nurs Health*, 22(4), 285–293.

Nehls, N. (2000). Being a case manager for persons with borderline personality disorder: perspectives of community mental health center clinicians. *Archives of Psychiatric Nursing*, 14(1), 12–18.

Searight, H.R. (1992). Borderline personality disorder: diagnosis and management in primary care. *The Journal of Family Practice*, 34(5), 605–612.

World Health Organisation (1992). *International Classification D10*. Classification of mental and behavioural disorders. Washington, DC: World Health Organisation.

Review of Chapter 2

Please circle your answer to each of the following:

How much of the chapter did you read?

0%   25%   50%   75%   100%

Overall, was it

Very helpful   Helpful   Don't know   Unhelpful

Comments

How the problems develop

HOW BORDERLINE PROBLEMS DEVELOP

There are a number of models of BPD described by psychologists and psychiatrists who work with people with borderline problems and carry out research to try and improve our understanding of it. This chapter will outline some of these models in order to help you understand how your problems developed. Personality traits or temperament are inherited and these can make someone vulnerable to developing BPD (Paris, 1998) and other psychological disorders. People with BPD have a 'labile' or reactive temperament (i.e. they have extreme emotional responses). The problems of most, but not all people with BPD, also result from the effects of severe or chronic trauma in childhood.

IS IT MORE COMMON IN WOMEN?

About three-quarters of people diagnosed as having BPD are women (Widiger and Frances, 1989). Men with BPD are more likely to be in substance abuse services and the criminal justice system. Women with borderline problems have experiences and problems such as sexual exploitation, dependency in relationships, identity problems, which are similar to but more severe than those of many women. Women with such problems are more likely to be given a psychiatric diagnosis than men with the same problems (Gunderson and Zanarini, 1987; Becker, 1997).

CHILDHOOD TRAUMA AND ITS EFFECTS

From two-thirds (Paris *et al.*, 1994) to over 90 per cent (Zanarini *et al.*, 1997) of people with borderline problems report a traumatic childhood in which they were either emotionally, physically or sexually abused. People who go on to develop BPD have usually experienced persistent maltreatment and neglect, though BPD may be finally triggered by a traumatic event or series of events (Zanarini and Frankenburg, 1997). Weaver and Clum (1993) suggest sexual abuse is the important aspect of the childhood experience of someone who develops borderline problems. Zanarini *et al.* (1997) found that experiences of neglect have more impact on the development of BPD than childhood sexual abuse.

In the face of overwhelming trauma, particularly during infancy or early childhood, we use simple defence mechanisms such as splitting off memories and experiences from conscious awareness. This is known as *dissociation*. The problems of many people with BPD are partly the consequence of the trauma they experienced as children and include, for example, detachment or estrangement from oneself or *depersonalisation*. This is when you have the sense of being outside your body or it feels unreal, or as if you are observing yourself. Some people hurt themselves in order to help bring them back to their body and the present moment. The external world can also feel strange or unreal. This is known as *derealisation*. These experiences do not mean you are going crazy but are usually the result of trauma. (They can also happen when you are intoxicated with or withdrawing from drugs or alcohol.) Numbing emotional pain is achieved through a number of defences including denial ('it never happened'), dissociation (blocking out feelings and memories), projection ('it's you not me') and minimising ('it happened but so what'). People with borderline problems can also have periods of psychosis or thought disorder. These are usually triggered by acute stress and improve in short periods of time without anti-psychotic medication. (This is the most recent criteria for BPD added to the DSM-IV.)

Layden *et al.* (1993) highlight the importance of taking account of the senses (touch, sound, sight, smell, etc.) involved in trauma, which vary at different stages of child development. Experiences in infancy will be via touch and sound such as tone of voice. Many people with borderline problems have difficulty in defining their emotions and thoughts associated with these early experiences. The memories may be held in sensations such as touch, tone of voice and fragmented images. Children who have experienced neglect or abuse in infancy will not have words for their feelings about those experiences. They may be linked instead to physical reactions such as feeling sick, becoming numb, or 'spaced out'. Memories which you can put into words are likely to be from mid- to late childhood. If you have strange physical sensations or you experience depersonalisation, using verbal strategies may not work for you. You may need to work with images, dreams and touch. Remember to discuss this in your sessions.

I'M NOT SURE MY CHILDHOOD WAS TRAUMATIC

People with borderline problems who do not report abuse or neglect may have had similar experiences in infancy before they acquired language. They also have high levels of dissociation and may have blocked these memories out. Some clients who do not report their parents as neglectful or abusive describe their parents as authoritarian or controlling. However, not all people with BPD have been abused and it is unhelpful to blame your past or family entirely for your problems.

In people who do not report a traumatic childhood, biological factors may be greater. It is unclear what the biological factors may be – possibly decreased serotonin (Coccaro *et al.*, 1989; Korzekwa *et al.*, 1993; Hollander *et al.*, 1994), but the cause of this is unknown and such changes are common to other conditions, notably depression. Whether acquired through trauma, modelling or biology, clear differences in emotional responses of people with borderline problems can be observed. Their emotional arousal is quicker and more intense and takes longer to return to baseline. People with borderline problems have genuine difficulty managing emotions and few skills in regulating them. This skill deficiency is much more comprehensive than for people with psychological problems affecting one or two areas. Like the treatment programme Linehan developed, this manual aims to help you develop these skills.

EMOTIONAL DYSREGULATION

Linehan (1993) suggests that it is constant *invalidation* rather than trauma which contributes to the development of BPD. This involves the invalidation of what the child says, does and even what they experience. Parental figures were inconsistent or punitive to the child when they were in pain or distressed. They may also have oversimplified solutions or had inappropriate expectations of what the child should be able to do. When parental figures behave like this over long periods it is because they severely lack parenting skills and may have had similar responses from their own parents. However, not all children who have such experiences develop borderline problems. Linehan gives a convincing account of how invalidating experiences interact with biological *'emotional dysregulation'*, and the extent of each influence will vary between individuals.

CORE BELIEFS

Young (1994) suggests that BPD results from early experience which leads to multiple, problematic core beliefs about oneself, others, the future or the world. He also recognises the role of temperament. These core beliefs stem from painful experiences which interfere with key tasks at different stages of child development (Layden *et al.*, 1993). These experiences undermine the achievement of the important tasks of adolescence, such as the establishment of a personal identity and life choices. It is at this time that borderline problems emerge.

INSECURITY IN RELATIONSHIPS

Finally, another model which is helpful in understanding borderline problems is attachment theory (Bowlby, 1969). Bowlby described the infant's innate tendency to seek closeness and maintain a bond with its mother. The pattern of our attachment, and in particular how secure it is, depends on the quality of parenting we receive. When attachment is secure the child learns how to tolerate separation. If not, a pattern of distress will be established which can result in problems in adulthood (Bowlby, 1977). BPD can be understood as a condition of profound insecure attachment with extreme swings between a desire for closeness but a dread of what this might lead to, and an expectation of abandonment (Sable, 1997; Fonagy *et al.*, 2000).

EXERCISES

The following exercises will help you to explore what experiences you have had in your life that have contributed to your problems.

E X E R C I S E **3.1** Construct a *family tree* linking all members of your extended family – your parents, their partners or spouses and all their children and your grandparents. Write the ages of everyone and mark when they died if any of them have.

Share this in your sessions. What are the important events in your family's history? What happened in your mother's and father's life? Can you see any patterns within the family? What different roles do members of the family tend to have? Are there different roles for men and women?

EXERCISE **3.2** *Home study* **Life line**

This exercise may distress you. Make sure you have a plan of how you will cope if you feel very distressed. Draw a long line and write all the important events of your life along the top especially those which were painful or traumatic for you. Then underneath write how each experience affected you. Alternatively, write your *life story*. You may find it easier to write as if you were writing about someone else.

REFERENCES

Becker, D. (1997). *Through the looking glass. Women and Borderline Personality Disorder.* Boulder, Colo.: Westview Press.

Bowlby, J. (1969). *Attachment.* New York: Basic Books.

Bowlby, J. (1977). The making and breaking of affectional bonds. *British Journal of Psychiatry*, 130, 201–210, 421–431.

Coccaro, E.F., Siever, L.J., Klar, H.M., Maurer, G., Cochrane, K., Cooper, T.B., Mohs, R.C. and Davis, K.L. (1989). Serotonergic studies in patients with affective and personality disorders: correlates with suicidal and impulsive, aggressive behaviour. *Archives of General Psychiatry*, 46, 587–599.

Fonagy, P., Target, M. and Gergely, G. (2000). Attachment and borderline personality disorder: a theory and some evidence. *Psychiatric Clinics of North America*, 23(1), 103–122.

Gunderson, J. and Zanarini, M. (1987). Pathogenesis of borderline personality. *Review of Psychiatry*, 8, 25–48.

Hamer, D. and Copeland, P. (2000) Living with our genes: why they matter more than you think. Macmillan.

Hollander, E., Stein, D.J., DeCaria, C.M., Cohen, L., Saoud, J.B., Skodol, A.E., Kellman, D., Rosnick, L. and Oldham, J.M. (1994). Serotonergic sensitivity in borderline personality disorder: Preliminary findings. *American Journal of Psychiatry*, 151, 277–280.

Korzekwa, M., Links, P. and Steiner, M. (1993). Biological markers in borderline personality disorder: new perspectives. *Canadian Journal of Psychiatry*, 38, S11–15.

Layden, M.A., Newman, C.F., Freeman, A. and Byers Morse, S. (1993). *Cognitive Therapy of Borderline Personality Disorder.* Boston, Mass.: Allyn & Bacon.

Linehan, M.M. (1993). *Cognitive Behaviour Therapy for Borderline Personality Disorder.* New York: Guilford Press.

Paris, J., Zweig-Frank, H. and Gudzer, J. (1994). Psychological risk factors for borderline personality disorder in female patients. *Comprehensive Psychiatry*, 35, 301–305.

Paris, J. (1998). Does childhood trauma cause personality disorders in adults? *Canadian Journal of Psychiatry*, 43, 148–153.

Sable, P. (1997) Attachment, detachment and borderline personality disorder. *Psychotherapy*, 34, 171–181.

Weaver, T.L. and Clum, G.A. (1993). Early family environments and the traumatic experiences associated with borderline personality disorder. *Journal of Consulting and Clinical Psychology*, 61, 1068–1075.

Widiger, T.A. and Frances, A.J. (1989). Epidemiology, diagnosis and comorbidity of borderline personality disorder. In A. Tasman, R.E. Hales and A.J. Frances (eds), *Review of Psychiatry*, Vol. 8, Washington, DC: American Psychiatric Press.

Young, J.E. (1994). *Cognitive Therapy for Personality Disorders: A Schema-focussed Approach* (revised edition). Sarasota, Fl.: Professional Resources Press.

Zanarini, M.C. and Frankenburg, F.R. (1997). Pathways to the development of borderline personality disorder. *Journal of Personality Disorders*, 11(1), 93–104.

Zanarini, M.C., Williams, A.A., Lewis, R.E., Reich, R.B., Vera, S.C., Marino, M.F. and Levin, A. (1997). Reported pathological childhood experiences associated with the development of BPD. *American Journal of Psychiatry*, 154, 1101–1106.

Review of Chapter 3

Please circle your answer to each of the following:

How much of the chapter did you read?

0%   25%   50%   75%   100%

Overall, was it

Very helpful   Helpful   Not relevant to me   Don't know   Unhelpful

Did you/your client complete Exercise 3.1?

Yes   No

Was it

Very helpful   Helpful   Don't know   Unhelpful

Did you/your client complete Exercise 3.2?

Yes   No

Was it

Very helpful   Helpful   Don't know   Unhelpful

Comments

Foundations for living well

In order to overcome your problems and reduce your suffering, you need to learn how to take care of yourself and live well. An important principle in this programme is that you are precious. You matter. You deserve to be well looked after. Taking care of yourself in any area of your life will have an effect on how you feel, your emotions, states of mind and your self-image. For example, eating regular meals and a healthy diet not only gives you nutritional food but is a direct way of monitoring your needs and looking after yourself. Such regular habits help to give us a structure and sense of purpose to our day. Many people with borderline problems lack such structure. You may have grown up in a family where there was not enough structure or, alternatively, where the structure was imposed rigidly or harshly so that you rebelled against it. Now you are an adult it is very important for you to be able to build your own structures – not as rigid rules but to ensure that your basic needs are met.

YOUR BODY IS PRECIOUS, TREAT IT WITH CARE

Try and eat three meals a day which include four or five portions of fruit and vegetables (preferably fresh) and some first-class protein. These are meat, fish, dairy products or vegan substitutes such as quorn or tofu. Fish is especially nutritious and has omega 3 fatty acids which are important to mental health. Whole cereals (wholemeal bread, pasta, brown rice, etc.) are more nutritious than refined foods and provide fibre, which is important for our health. These are known as complex carbohydrates and give you energy over a sustained period of time compared to simple carbohydrates, such as white sugar and white flour products (cakes, biscuits, chocolate, etc.), which burn up more quickly and can lead to fluctuations in blood sugar levels and craving. Caffeine in drinks can have a similar effect. Regular eating habits are especially important if you have an eating problem and (in women) when you are premenstrual. This may be difficult for you to achieve if you have been undereating or eating chaotically. You may need to make changes gradually. Keeping a food diary for a while and sharing this in your sessions could be useful.

EXERCISE **4.1**

Do you eat a balanced diet of healthy foods?

Do you eat regular meals?

Do you think you need to improve your diet? If so, what realistic goals could you set yourself?

WORK, REST AND PLAY

These are basic human needs and we probably need them in similar proportions. If you don't have a job and aren't raising children it could be helpful for you to do voluntary work or pursue an interest through further education. This helps build your skills and confidence. (If you need support to achieve this discuss this with your guide.) Research shows that unemployment contributes to depression and poor mental and physical health.

Rest may not be something you prioritise. Maybe you stay up late if you feel like it, run on all cylinders for a few days then crash out. How do you relax?

Routines may seem boring, but they really help to ensure we look after ourselves. Generally it's a good idea to go to bed at a reasonable time (by midnight) and get up by 8 or 9 a.m. Most people need about 7–8 hours sleep a night. If you get strung out and exhausted this will compound your problems (e.g. contribute to you being irritable and having a short fuse).

If you sleep badly consider the following:

⊙ Give up caffeinated drinks in the evening. If you drink tea or coffee have decaffeinated. Chocolate and tobacco are also stimulants.
⊙ Alcohol disrupts our sleep. It can wake you up to use the loo because it's a diuretic. Also having sedated you, when this effect wears off you are likely to wake up.
⊙ Have a routine to prepare for sleep. You need to relax and not stimulate the mind. If your mind is alert you will need to do something to calm it down.
⊙ If you think about things you have to do, problems or tend to worry, try writing them down. Then clear your mind and think of something neutral or pleasant.
⊙ Try visualising and counting games to still and occupy your mind. They can help you to slip into sleep.

E X E R C I S E **4.2** How do you spend your time? What's a typical day like for you?

How do you have fun?!

How could you have more fun?

What realistic goals could you set yourself?

EXERCISE

Exercise is important for mental well-being and there is evidence that it can have more lasting benefit in overcoming depression than anti-depressants. Also, people who maintain a healthy weight are likely to do so by regular exercise. (Dieting is rarely successful in maintaining weight loss.) Exercise needs to be regular and kept up over a long time. This means that you need to enjoy it and build it into your routine. It doesn't have to be an intense workout and you don't have to feel exhausted (e.g. walking is a very effective form of exercise, especially if it is brisk).

EXERCISE **4.3**   What exercise do you enjoy?

If you don't exercise regularly, what could you do and when?

MENTAL AND SPIRITUAL WELL-BEING

These are also important qualities in our lives. This doesn't necessarily mean going to church, but having a personal philosophy and meaning to your life. This can really help when you are having a hard time. There are many teachings and faiths which you may find helpful. It is especially important that you know how to feel tranquil and peaceful without having to drink or take drugs. This may come from relaxation or meditation, or from being in the countryside if you are near green spaces. If you live in a town or a city you can sit on a bench in a park, walk amongst trees or contemplate a flower in a garden. When you are indoors music can be helpful in finding calm and serenity as well as excitement!

Mental well-being comes from living in a way which is, as far as possible, harmless to others and yourself. The more generosity and understanding you can cultivate towards yourself and others the happier you will tend to feel. This is for *your* benefit, not anyone else.

E X E R C I S E **4.4** Notice the relationship between what you do, how you are to others and yourself and how you feel. For example, how do you feel after watching a violent film? Record some examples (things that you make you feel good and things that make you feel bad).

Do you have a philosophy or spiritual faith?

What activities help you to feel calm and nourished?

Do you need to practise these more often? If so when would be a good time?

THE COMPANY YOU KEEP

Related to mental and spiritual well-being is the company you keep. What effect do different people have on you? If your life changes for the better this may mean that you will mix with different people. This is especially important if you use illegal drugs and alcohol. It will be harder for you to give these up if you spend time around others who use them regularly or think it's OK. It is important for you to make friends with people who will try and support you in tackling your problems. There are a number of ways you can meet such people. If you have had a drink or drug problem, AA or NA may be helpful.

EXERCISE **4.5** Make a list of the people you see most often.

Do they misuse drugs or alcohol?

Are they generally loyal to their friends?

Do you feel cared for and supported in your friendships?

Any thoughts about this?

To achieve things you have to be able to work at them and may not reap the benefit immediately. People with borderline problems do not find this easy. They tend to do what they feel like doing. Many have backgrounds where self-discipline and effort have not been modelled or where it has been imposed harshly. Experiment with planning to structure your day differently and see how that feels. Making goals and keeping them is a vital part of getting on in the world. This is an area that may not come easily to you or may have been disrupted by your life experience. It will be important for you to address this if you want to benefit from this programme.

EXERCISE **4.6** What do you associate with structure?

What gets in the way of you setting or achieving goals?

Do you think you need more structure in your life?

If so, in what way?

Life is like the sea and we are a boat getting tossed around! The hull is what keeps us afloat. Look over this chapter. What is in your hull? Get two colour pens or pencils. Write in what you have (good friends, physical health, etc.). What else would you like to put in? Add these in a different colour.

MAKING A COMMITMENT TO THE PROGRAMME

Some of your problems may directly interfere with attempts at change being successful – for example, impulsiveness leading to unskilful behaviour, relationship problems, losing hope and faith. In order to work these through it is very important that you make a commitment to the programme. This means:

⊙ reading the manual – which may not happen unless you set aside a regular time and try to stick to it;
⊙ attending the support or supervision sessions;
⊙ contacting the service if you are not going to make the session;
⊙ keeping a diary in the format suggested (this will vary), and carrying out other agreed tasks;
⊙ making a commitment to avoid using illegal drugs and alcohol, harming yourself or attempting suicide – you are unlikely to learn other ways of coping whilst using these strategies.

Note that there will be times when you don't want to do some of these things (or all of them!). However, feelings are not a good basis for action!

EXERCISE **4.8** Will any of these get in the way of you following this programme, or sabotage your efforts to tackle your problems?

⊙ not reading the manual
⊙ not believing in yourself
⊙ not doing the exercises
⊙ not believing in those providing the programme
⊙ not keeping the diaries

Can you think of anything you can do to try and prevent this?

PROFESSIONAL HELP AND MEDICATION

You may benefit from medication, particularly if you have problems with consistently low mood (not just fluctuating periods of depression). Traditional anti-depressants (tricyclics) or tranquilisers (benzodiazepines) are not generally recommended as they can increase your impulsiveness and loss of control. Also, toxic drugs such as tricyclic anti-depressants should be avoided for people at risk of overdosing. Modern anti-depressants (SSRIs such as fluoxetine [Prozac], sertraline or paroxetine, or SSRI-related drugs such as venlafaxine) can be helpful in moderating your mood (Cornelius *et al.*, 1990; Coccaro *et al.*, 1990). They may also help reduce self-harm (Cornelius *et al.*, 1991; Markovitz *et al.*, 1991; Verkes *et al.*, 1998), anger (Kavoussi *et al.*, 1994; Salzman *et al.*, 1995) and aggressive behaviour (Coccaro and Kavoussi, 1997). They may be helpful even if you are not depressed (Markovitz *et al.*, 1991). However, they are unlikely to change feelings of emptiness, boredom and frustration. A herbal medicine called hypericum, or St John's wort, is also an effective anti-depressant (Linde and Mulrow, 1998). You can buy this yourself, but it may be better to consult a medical herbalist.

Carbamazepine may be helpful in managing anger or lack of control (Cowdry and Gardner, 1988; Hollander *et al.*, 2001) but can increase depression (Gardner and Cowdry, 1986). Lamotrigine may be helpful for people with mood swings (Pinto and Akiskal, 1998). Low doses of neuroleptics (such as phenelzine) can help reduce irritability, anger, suspicion or paranoid thinking (Soloff *et al.*, 1993; Hori, 1998), but research findings vary. However, they have been associated with higher levels of depression and excess sleep (Cornelius *et al.*, 1993), and patients may not tolerate the side effects. MAOIs can improve anger and impulse control (Cowdry and Gardner, 1988). Lithium may help reduce aggression (Hori, 1998) but, again, research findings vary (Tupin *et al.*, 1973; Sheard *et al.*, 1976).

In conclusion, medication does not directly treat BPD, but can be helpful in the short- to medium-term management of problems. It is important for you to try medication long enough for you to judge whether you get any benefit. A minimum of two weeks is often needed before you feel the effect and for side effects to wear off.

EXERCISE **4.9**

Have you been prescribed medication and if so do you take it as advised?

Are there any questions you would like to ask of your GP or psychiatrist?

Do you need to have your medication reviewed?

Discuss your concerns in your sessions.

REFERENCES

Coccaro, E.F., Astill, J.L., Herbert, J.L. *et al.* (1990). Fluoxetine treatment of impulsive aggression in DSM-III-R personality disorder patients. *Journal of Clinical Psychopharmacology*, 10, 373–375.

Coccaro, E.F. and Kavoussi, R.J. (1997). Fluoxetine and impulsive aggressive behaviour in personality disordered subjects. *Archives of General Psychiatry*, 54, 1081–1088.

Cornelius, J.R., Soloff, P.H., Perel, J.M. *et al.* (1990). Fluoxetine trial in borderline personality disorder. *Psychopharmacology Bulletin*, 26, 151–154.

Cornelius, J.R., Soloff, P.H., Perel, J.M. and Ulrich, R.F. (1991). A preliminary trial of fluoxetine in refractory borderline patients. *Journal of Clinical Psychopharmacology*, 11(2), 116–120.

Cornelius, J.R., Soloff, P.H., Perel, J.M. and Ulrich, R.F. (1993). Continuation pharmacotherapy of borderline personality disorder with haloperidol and phenelzine. *American Journal of Psychiatry*, 150(12), 1843–1848.

Cowdry, R. and Gardner, D.L. (1988). Pharmacotherapy of borderline personality disorder. *Archives of General Psychiatry*, 45, 111–119.

Gardner, D.L. and Cowdry, R. (1986). Positive effects of carbamazepine on behavioral dyscontrol in borderline personality disorder. *American Journal of Psychiatry*, 143, 519–522.

Hollander, E., Allen, A., Lopez, R.P., Bienstock, C.A., Grossman, R., Siever, L.J., Merkatz, L. and Stein, D.J. (2001). A preliminary double-blind, placebo-controlled trial of divalproex sodium in borderline personality disorder. *Journal of Clinical Psychiatry*, 62, 199–203.

Hori, A. (1998). Pharmacotherapy for personality disorders. *Psychiatry and Clinical Neuroscience*, 52, 13–19.

Kavoussi, R.J., Liu, J. and Coccaro, E.F. (1994). An open trial of sertraline in personality disordered patients with impulsive aggression. *Journal of Clinical Psychiatry*, 55, 137–141.

Linde, K. and Mulrow, C.D. (1998). St. John's wort for depression. *Cochrane Review*, July. In the Cochrane Library. Oxford: Update Software.

Markovitz, P.J., Calabrese, J.R., Schulz, S.C. and Meltzer, H.Y. (1991). Fluoxetine in the treatment of borderline and schizotypal personality disorders. *American Journal of Psychiatry*, 148, 1064–1067.

Pinto, O.C. and Akiskal, H.S. (1998). Lamotrigine as a promising approach to borderline personality: an open case series without concurrent DSM-IV major mood disorder. *Journal of Affective Disorders*, 51, 333–343.

Salzman, C., Wolfson, A.N., Schatzberg, A. *et al.* (1995). Effect of fluoxetine on anger in symptomatic volunteers with borderline personality disorder. *Journal of Clinical Psychopharmacology*, 15, 23–29.

Sheard, M.H., Marini, J.L., Bridges, C.I. *et al.* (1976). The effect of lithium on unipolar aggressive behavior in man. *American Journal of Psychiatry*, 133, 1409–1413.

Soloff, P.H. (2000). Psychopharmacology of borderline personality disorder. *Psychiatric Clinics of North America*, 23, 169–192.

Soloff, P.H., Cornelius, J., George, A., Nathan, S., Perel, J.M. and Ulrich, R.F. (1993). Efficacy of phenelzine and haloperidol in borderline personality disorder. *Archives of General Psychiatry*, 50, 377–385.

Tupin, J.P., Smith, D.B., Clanon, T.L., Kim, L.I., Nugent, A. and Groupe, A. (1973). The long-term use of lithium in aggressive prisoners. *Comprehensive Psychiatry*, 14, 311–317.

Verkes, R.J., Van de Mast, R.C., Kerkhof, A.J., Fekkes, D., Hengeveld, M.W., Tyul, J.P. and Van Kempen, G.M. (1998). Platelet serotonin, monoamine oxidase activity, and [3H] paroxetine binding related to impulsive suicide attempts and borderline personality disorder. *Biological Psychiatry*, 43, 740–746.

FURTHER READING

Lindenfield, G. (1996). *Self Motivation*. London: Thorsons.

Review of Chapter 4

Please circle your answer to each of the following:

How much of the chapter did you read?

0%   25%   50%   75%   100%

Overall, was it

Very helpful   Helpful   Not relevant to me   Don't know   Unhelpful

Did you/your client complete Exercise 4.1?

Yes   No

Was it

Very helpful   Helpful   Don't know   Unhelpful

Did you/your client complete Exercise 4.2?

Yes   No

Was it

Very helpful   Helpful   Don't know   Unhelpful

Did you/your client complete Exercise 4.3?

Yes   No

Was it

Very helpful   Helpful   Don't know   Unhelpful

Did you/your client complete Exercise 4.4?

Yes   No

Was it

Very helpful   Helpful   Don't know   Unhelpful

Did you/your client complete Exercise 4.5?

Yes   No

Was it

Very helpful   Helpful   Don't know   Unhelpful

Did you/your client complete Exercise 4.6?

Yes   No

Was it

Very helpful   Helpful   Don't know   Unhelpful

Did you/your client complete Exercise 4.7?

Yes   No

Was it

Very helpful   Helpful   Don't know   Unhelpful

Did you/your client complete Exercise 4.8?

Yes   No

Was it

Very helpful   Helpful   Don't know   Unhelpful

Did you/your client complete Exercise 4.9?

Yes   No

Was it

Very helpful   Helpful   Don't know   Unhelpful

Comments

How you use drugs and alcohol

Most of us use alcohol to relax and have fun and caffeine to keep us alert. Alcohol and drugs, however, are dangerous when used to excess or used regularly to cope with negative emotional states. Over 50 per cent of people with BPD have problems with drugs and alcohol (Trull *et al.*, 2000), and overcoming this improves recovery (Links *et al.*, 1995). You may use drugs or alcohol for a number of reasons – to get in with a crowd, to 'get out of it' or to 'get a fix'. Or maybe because you are bored or feel life is empty, or to block out painful feelings or memories. What is your pattern of use? You need to examine this honestly, with someone you can trust who is impartial (i.e. not getting drunk or using illegal drugs themselves).

Home study diary of substance use

Keep a diary of when you take drugs or alcohol. Can you identify a pattern of use?

Do you try to escape from particular feelings or emotional states? If so, can you describe what these states are like?

If you regularly get drunk or take drugs, does it help you to

⊙ Get high? . . .
⊙ Escape from boredom? . . .

⊙ Get in with other people? . . .
⊙ Forget painful memories? . . .
⊙ Numb difficult feelings? . . .

How else could you get this/these?

If you are willing to try alternatives, this programme will help you. Discuss in sessions what these might be. It won't be easy for you to learn these while you continue to drink heavily or regularly take street drugs.

ASSESSING YOUR USE OF ALCOHOL

Health guidelines suggest women should not consume more than 14 units of alcohol per week and men more than 21. A unit is a small glass of wine, a short, or half a pint of beer or lager. This means two drinks per day maximum for women and three for men. It is a good idea to not drink alcohol or use illegal drugs on a daily basis. If you do it will increase your tolerance and tend to make you drink or take more in order to get the same effect. If you get 'the shakes' in the morning, needing a drink to steady you, then you are physically dependent. (This is the beginning of alcohol withdrawal.) If this happens, you will almost certainly need specialist help to tackle your alcohol problem. Psychological dependence is much more common. This is when you rely on alcohol to manage your life or cope with problems.

COMMON PROBLEMS CAUSED BY ALCOHOL

⊙ *Effects on your mind*: poor concentration, forgetfulness, memory problems from chronic, severe alcohol use, slow reaction times, muddled thinking.
⊙ *Effects on your feelings*: depression, irritability, hostility, hopelessness, despair.
⊙ *Effects on behaviour*: arguments, difficulty getting things done at work and home, carelessness and increased accidents, difficulty getting up and keeping commitments, secretive behaviour, telling lies to yourself and others.
⊙ *Effects on your body*: loss of appetite, dehydration, disturbed sleep later in the night, loss of interest in sex and difficulty getting sexually aroused, headaches, nausea and vomiting, poor co-ordination and clumsiness, blurred vision, dizziness.

You may not drink alcohol or use drugs daily, but when you do, you drink until you are drunk or pass out. Whilst this is common for young people it can be very dangerous for a number of reasons. You may get alcohol or drug poisoning and can die. When you are drunk or have taken illegal drugs you may not be in full control of yourself and have a serious or life-threatening accident. You may be a risk to others if you drive a car or are prone to violent anger. If you have young children you will not be able to take care of them or protect them. Finally, when you are under the influence of drugs or drunk you are vulnerable to harm or exploitation by others. Women may be used for sex, especially if others around are using drugs or drinking.

E X E R C I S E **5.2** If you drink heavily or use drugs you probably enjoy this and find it helps you to escape from unpleasant states of mind. You may not feel ready to think about giving them up or even reducing them. This exercise will help you explore that decision.

If you take illegal drugs, try to complete an analysis of the pros and cons of change:

Benefits of taking drugs	Costs and disadvantages of taking drugs (e.g. cost)
Benefits of giving up drugs	Risks and possible losses if I change

If you regularly get drunk or use alcohol to manage your feelings, what are the pros and cons of change?

Benefits of getting drunk	Costs and disadvantages of getting drunk (e.g. cost, increased hostility and violence) What problems has my drinking caused so far? To me? To others? What problems might it cause if I carry on?
Benefits of only drinking moderately	Risks and possible losses if I change

Now go back and underline the ones that are really important to you.

EXERCISE 5.3

Goals for change

If you feel ready to reduce your use of drugs or alcohol, how could you begin to do this?

What changes would you need to make to help support you in this?

If you're afraid of doing this, could you try going for a period of time without alcohol or drugs or going to a club without taking drugs? Continue to keep the diary and talk over in sessions how you got on.

REFERENCES

Links, P.S., Heslegrave, R.J., Mitton, J.E. *et al.* (1995). Borderline personality disorder and substance misuse: consequences of comorbidity. *Canadian Journal of Psychiatry*, 40, 9–14.

Trull, T.J., Sher, K.J., Minks-Brown, C., Durbin, J. and Burr, R. (2000). Borderline personality disorder and substance abuse disorders: a review and integration. *Clinical Psychology Review*, 20(2), 235–253.

FURTHER READING

Ellis, A. and Velton, E. (1992). *When AA Doesn't Work for You*. Fort Lee, N.J.: Barricade Books.

Horvath, A.T. (1998). *Sex, Drugs, Gambling and Chocolate: A Workbook for Overcoming Addictions*. San Luis Obispo, Calif.: Impact Publishers Inc.

Kathleen, S. (1997). *Pocket Guide to the 12 Steps*. Freedom, Calif.: The Crossing Press.

Miller, S.D. and Berg, I.K. (1997). *The Miracle Method. A Radically New Approach to Problem Drinking*. London: Brief Therapy Press.

Review of Chapter 5

Please circle your answer to each of the following:

How much of the chapter did you read?

0%   25%   50%   75%   100%

Overall, was it

Very helpful   Helpful   Not relevant to me   Don't know   Unhelpful

Did you/your client complete Exercise 5.1?

Yes   No

Was it

Very helpful   Helpful   Don't know   Unhelpful

Did you/your client complete exercise 5.2?

Yes   No

Was it

Very helpful   Helpful   Don't know   Unhelpful

Did you/your client complete Exercise 5.3?

Yes   No

Was it

Very helpful   Helpful   Don't know   Unhelpful

Comments

CHAPTER 6

Understanding and managing emotions

UNDERSTANDING EMOTIONS

All human beings have emotional problems – times when they feel despair, anger, disappointment, envy, boredom, restlessness, agitation. It is a myth that people diagnosed with a psychiatric disorder are emotionally disturbed while everyone else is OK! (People with mental health problems may feel worse, these feelings persist longer and they find it harder to function in daily life.) Here are some basic truths about emotions:

⊙ Everyone suffers.
⊙ Emotions, like other conditions (such as the weather, the physical state of our body, even the state of the planet), change.
⊙ Emotional distress is caused partly by real external experience (loss, poverty, injustice) and partly by the perspective we take and views we hold (e.g. taking things personally).

We all 'lose it' at times and get carried away with an emotional state. When people with borderline problems 'lose it' the consequences can be more severe – they may do things which are self-destructive or destructive of others. What is it that we lose? It is not easy to capture this in a single word. Can you think of what words would best describe what it is you have when you are emotionally calm, flexible (not driven, strung out, confused, overwhelmed)? Let's call it mindfulness or awareness. More about this later.

EMOTIONAL ROLLER-COASTERING

Joel Paris, a specialist in BPD, describes the emotional life of people with borderline problems as like being on a roller-coaster (Paris, 1994). There are a number of factors which we know contribute to overwhelming emotional states and lead to many mental health problems (depression, anxiety, etc., as well as 'personality disorders'):

1 *Real emotional experiences which were overwhelming* (see Chapters 3 and 9). Most people with borderline problems have experienced enduring trauma in childhood.
2 *Greater extremes in emotions and high emotional arousal.* (This may be caused by such experience, but may also be biologically influenced.) If Jo Average experiences emotional changes like so:

then someone with borderline problems would experience emotional changes like so:

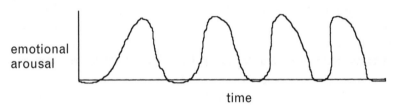

i.e. more extreme highs and lows and more rapid changes. Also, it takes longer for their emotional state to settle back to normal. Jo Average's emotional arousal would look like this:

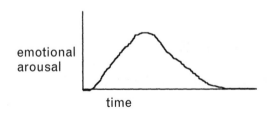

Someone with borderline problems would look like this:

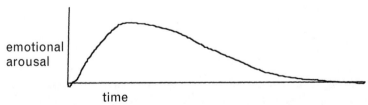

3 *Lack of skills in regulating emotion*. People with borderline problems have not learnt healthy ways of managing emotions. You may have had role models who couldn't regulate their own emotions (e.g. an alcoholic or disturbed parent). Parental figures may have had caretakers who invalidated you. It is difficult to learn to manage your emotions when they are denied or dismissed by the adults we grow up with.

These factors can reinforce each other. For example, if you have been neglected or abandoned (1), certain experiences are likely to be difficult for you, such as being alone or at times when you feel let down. This may trigger painful memories which cause you to be emotionally aroused (2). Not knowing how to cope with these feelings (3), you are likely to continue to feel upset and therefore more painful memories are triggered which you brood on or cannot easily distract yourself from (3).

Most people when they are upset feel it is beyond their control. You are also likely to feel that others are responsible for upsetting you. Those feelings may have been justified in the past, but it will not be helpful for you to always see your experience in that way. This is an important issue to discuss in sessions. If you think of yourself as a victim and others as the 'persecutor', it is important for you to recognise and try to re-evaluate this. Blaming yourself is not a better alternative. This is an example of what we call *black and white thinking*. It may feel or seem *as if* either 'It's my fault', 'I'm to blame' or 'I'm in the wrong', or 'It's their fault', 'They're to blame', 'They are in the wrong'. More about that in the next chapter.

DIFFERENT STATES[1]

Everybody experiences changes in how they feel about themselves and the world. For some people these changes are extreme, sudden or confusing. There may be a number of states that recur, and learning to recognise them and shifts between them can be very helpful.

---

[1] This is part of the psychotherapy file, a tool used in cognitive analytic therapy (Ryle, 1995).

E X E R C I S E **6.1**

(a) Below are a number of descriptions of difficult states. Identify those which you experience by circling them. You can delete or add words to the descriptions and there is a space to add any not listed.

Zombie. Cut off from feelings, cut off from others, disconnected
Feeling bad but soldiering on, coping
Out of control rage
Cheated by life, by others. Mistrustful
Provoking, teasing, seducing, winding-up others
Clinging, fearing abandonment
Frenetically active. Too busy to think or feel
Agitated, confused, anxious
Feeling perfectly cared for, blissfully close to another
Rejected, abandoned
Hate myself
Vulnerable, needy, passively helpless, waiting for rescue
Envious, wanting to harm others, put them down, pull them down
Hurting myself
Hurting others
Hurt, humiliated by others
Intensely critical of self
Intensely critical of others
Frightened of others

(b) During the next week make a note of which states you experience and what triggered them. Are there any others?

(c) Now put a cross by the five states which are most problematic for you. How do you cope with these different states? Write down what you tend to do when you are in each of these five states.

⊙

⊙

⊙

⊙

⊙

6.2 *Home study*

The first stage in managing your emotions more effectively is to know which emotional states are a problem for you, what tends to trigger them, and how you respond.

Keep a diary of difficult emotional states and how you manage them. This is a very important part of the programme. When you are not doing any other diary, you will need to continue to do this throughout the programme.

Management of Emotions Diary

Please complete as soon as possible every time you get upset. Try to identify exactly what emotion you experienced (this will help you detach a little from the feelings), then briefly describe how you dealt with it. Think about the consequences of what you did and whether it was destructive/unskilful or constructive/skilful. If this is not clear discuss it in sessions.

State or emotion	What you did	Was this skilful (S) or unskilful (U) (think about why?)	If unskilful, how could you have handled it better?
e.g. Lonely	Got drunk	U	Phoned and talked talked to someone
e.g. Angry	Went for a walk to cool off	S	

EXERCISE 6.3a Thinking about the worst states for you and what you tend to do when you get in them, make a list of your main emotional and behavioural problems. This will help you to be clear about what your problems are and which you think are the most important for you to tackle.

What order would you like to tackle them in? Put numbers against the list.

Having clear goals is important as there are going to be times when your motivation to work on your problems will flag. We all get demoralised and feel hopeless at times. You may feel angry with yourself or others that things aren't getting better quickly enough. You may feel you aren't getting the right help and want to express your anger by being destructive and sabotaging the work you have done. Your long-term goals will help motivate you to keep going at these times.

EXERCISE 6.3b How would you like your life to be better?

What do you think you need to learn or achieve to get there? How might you need to change?

SKILFUL MEANS: MINDFULNESS IS THE FIRST STEP

Mindfulness is subtle but it is something we can develop. It is now being taught to help people with a wide range of problems, including pain and depression. Thich Nhat Hanh (1991) describes how we can best approach the problem of emotional suffering:

When we have an unpleasant feeling we may want to chase it away. But it is more effective to return to our conscious breathing and just observe it, identifying it silently to ourselves. Calling a feeling by its name such as anger, sorrow, joy, happiness helps us identify it clearly and recognise it more deeply. We can use our breathing to be in contact with our feelings and accept them . . . The first step in dealing with feelings is to recognise each feeling as it arises. The agent that does this is mindfulness . . .

The second step is to become one with the feeling. It is best not to say 'Go away fear, I don't like you'. It is much more effective to say 'Hello fear, how are you today?' Then you can invite the two aspects of yourself, mindfulness and fear, to shake hands as friends and become one. Doing this may seem frightening but because you know that you are more than just your fear you need not be afraid. As long as mindfulness is there it can chaperone your fear. The fundamental practice is to nourish your mindfulness with conscious breathing, to keep it there alive and strong. Although your mindfulness may not be very powerful at the beginning, if you nourish it, it will become stronger.

The third step is to calm the feeling. As mindfulness is taking good care of your fear, you begin to calm down 'Breathing in I calm the activities of body and mind'. You calm your feeling just by being with it, like a mother tenderly holding her crying baby. The mother is your mindfulness and it will tend the feeling of pain . . .

The fourth step is to the release the feeling . . . to let it go. You look deeply . . . to see the cause of what is wrong. By looking you will see what will help you to transform the feeling . . . The therapist helps you see which kind of ideas and beliefs have led to your suffering. Many patients want to get rid of their painful feelings, but they do not want to get rid of their beliefs, the viewpoints that are the very root of their feelings . . . The same is true when we use mindfulness to transform our feelings. After recognising the feeling, becoming one with it calming it down and releasing it, we can look deeply into its causes which are often based on inaccurate perception.

When you know that you are capable of taking care of your fear, it is already reduced to a minimum, becoming softer and not so unpleasant. Now you can smile at it and let it go . . . You now have an opportunity to go deeper and work on transforming the source of your fear. The fifth step is to look deeply.

(Thich Nhat Hanh, 1991, pp. 51–54)

Identifying and accepting our feelings is difficult when these were invalidated. This process will take time and effort. These exercises will help.

6.4 *Home study* **mindfulness of breathing practice**

There are some times in the day when you can use your daily life as a cue to practise mindfulness (e.g. making a cup of tea). There is a well-known Zen saying 'When you walk just walk, when you eat just eat.' Choose one activity you do at least daily and make it a meditation practice. What will it be?

Share in sessions how you got on.

As you practise Exercise 6.4 your breathing will become more peaceful and this will help to calm your mind. Just breathing and smiling to ourselves can help us to feel better and be in the present moment. Once you have established this skill you can begin to use it when you are stressed or upset. However, you will only be able to do this if you practise it regularly – at least every day. After that, try to do it when you are mildly stressed or upset. When you have established that skill you can gradually use it when your emotions are more intense, but this will take time. Results will not be instant, but if you practise regularly you will feel the benefit.

Linehan (1993) describes mindfulness skills as:

⊙ skilful understanding (known in Zen as 'wise mind');
⊙ observing your mind and describing what's happening in your mind (this is anger . . . this shame . . . this is fear, etc.);
⊙ acting wisely, being non-judgemental, in-the-moment and effective (i.e. focusing on what works).

In order for you to cope better and not feel so overwhelmed by distress there are certain skills you have to develop. These include:

⊙ decreasing the emotional arousal associated with emotion;
⊙ re-orienting your attention away from the emotion;
⊙ inhibiting actions which are based on extreme emotional states, such as avoiding things because you are anxious, keeping things secret because you feel ashamed, being violent because you are angry;
⊙ experiencing emotions without escalating or compounding them or blocking them out;
⊙ planning what to do to achieve life goals.

EXERCISE **6.5**

What ideas do you have about how you could develop these skills?

You will find a list of examples at the end of the chapter. Talk through difficult times from your diary. Together think of all the steps you could have taken using mindfulness skills.

EXERCISE **6.6**

Home study **mindfulness practice**

Spend five minutes every day practising mindfulness of breathing. When you breathe in say to yourself 'in' and when you breathe out say 'out'. Agree in sessions the best time of the day for you to do this.

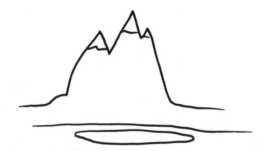

EXERCISE **6.7**

Applied mindfulness practice

What qualities would be helpful for you to develop?

What image captures that quality for you? A mountain could symbolise strength, or an image of a lake could help give you a sense of calm. When you practise mindfulness of breathing you can say to yourself, for example, 'mountain' as you breath in and 'strong' as you breath out.

THE MIDDLE WAY

Remember we have said that people with borderline problems tend to have a wide range of feelings (high and low) – particularly deep lows. They experience more extreme emotional states which can be triggered quickly. Once they are emotionally charged up it can take some time to return to 'baseline'. It isn't surprising that people with these intense and changing emotions tend to behave in similarly extreme ways – for example, drinking a whole bottle of spirits rather than just a few drinks or having sex with a stranger rather than feel lonely. Beck *et al.* (1990) suggest that mood swings are created by black-and-white thinking and that learning to rein this habit in will lessen mood swings considerably. There is an important rule of thumb which we will talk about a lot in this programme: 'the middle way'. This may sound boring, but finding the middle way in both your thoughts and actions will help you feel better, reduce your addictive habits and not put yourself at such risk.

EXERCISE 6.8

See if you can think of some of the things you feel or do to an extreme and then think of what the middle way might be. Here's an example:

Feel desperately lonely, long to be with someone	Get very involved with someone, then feel I lose my identity, or see so much of them I get bored

What would be a middle way between these two extremes?

Sometimes, too, it's as if we have restricted choices in our feelings or behaviour. For example, when things go wrong it's as if either

it's all my fault (you blame yourself)   or   it's all their fault (you blame them).

What would be a middle way between these two positions?

People learn to act out one end of this even if they feel both. Men are more likely to take their anger out on others while women, even if they feel anger towards others, are more likely to take their anger out on themselves. Practising mindfulness, staying with a feeling, will help you to develop the middle way.

Here are some more examples. What's the middle way?

Want to have a good time and forget all about my problems	Feel total despair and panic unless I get help immediately
Preoccupied with my appearance Buy a lot of clothes Change my hair style or colour	Neglect myself Don't take any interest in my physical appearance
Get really enthusiastic about something; do it a lot	Get bored quickly; give things up

Fall in love and think 'this is the one'	Go off someone quickly; can't stand their company
Go on a diet Ban high calorie foods	'Pig out' Binge on junk food
Try to be nice and please people all the time	Lose my temper; say nasty, hurtful things
Fancy someone; fantasise about being with them	Hate someone's guts; never want to see them again
Feel inadequate, inferior; try to be like someone else	Look down on people and despise them

Can you spot any more?

Can you see how the two extremes may be linked? One can lead to the other! For example, if you fall head over heels in love with someone you tend to set yourself up for a long fall. Inevitably the thrill and highs pass and you hit the disappointment, conflict or ordinariness in a relationship. Talk this over in sessions. You may be able to track a pattern in which one leads to the other. Or maybe it feels like you only have two choices – one extreme or the other (a 'dilemma').

What, if any, would you like to change? There will be many positions you can take between these extremes. Think of as many possibilities as you can.

E X E R C I S E **6.9** **Do this one in sessions**

Identify an area where you think in black-and-white ways (e.g. that people are either totally untrustworthy or totally trustworthy). Define each end of the pole. Then think how you would rate different people on those qualities. Draw a line between the two poles and put people on the line.

Is everyone one extreme or the other?

EXERCISE **6.10** *Home study* **taking things less personally**

We all identify with our emotions, 'lose ourselves' and take things personally.

(a) During the rest of today, try to notice every emotion you experience and give it a name. For example anger, disappointment, joy, irritation, restlessness, love.

Imagine a chart on the wall or a heap on the floor. Visualise adding each emotion to the chart or heap.

(b) One of the aims of this programme is to help you recognise your emotions and not avoid them or block them out, or blame anyone for them, including you! You may notice patterns to your emotions such as:

⊙ I often mistrust people. I get suspicious of people's motives.
⊙ I want everyone to like me, and feel anxious if they don't.
⊙ I have a problem about feeling let down.

Write down any patterns you notice:

Recognising such patterns helps us own the problem and accept that the problem is ours. When you are in a state and not mindful you can ask yourself 'Is it any of these habits?' It is important when you do this that you don't flip from projecting the problem outwards ('people are always letting me down', 'life is so unfair') to blaming yourself ('you're doing it again you stupid . . .').

MANAGING CRISES

You will inevitably find that at times you feel emotionally overwhelmed, and this may trigger a number of different states! Most people with borderline problems have a very low threshold for stress and can easily go into 'catastrophe' mode when things aren't going well. This may make you feel like the future is hopeless and you want to die.

E X E R C I S E **6.11** What is catastrophe mode like for you?

What sends you into crisis?

How do you manage crises?

You will not be able to change this until you have practised other coping skills, which hopefully you will do throughout the programme. You will need to 'cue' yourself into coping/problem-solving mode. There are a number of ways you can do this. You can use a written statement or 'cue card' which is a commitment to yourself to manage differently. You can wear an elastic band and ping it lightly (it is not to hurt yourself with) when you notice you are in catastrophe mode. This will help you be aware of how you are responding and the fact that you could respond differently. If you have a spiritual faith you can wear something to hold in times of need. This can help to centre you and give you a sense of inner strength. Alternatively, you could carry a list of possible things to do to manage the situation more skilfully. This is not a magic answer but something you will have to cultivate and work at. Discuss this at regular intervals in sessions and review, amend and add to your list of possible coping actions.

E X E R C I S E **6.12** When you are in a jam ask yourself the following questions. Practise doing this in sessions over a situation that happened recently.

- ⊙ In what other ways can I view the situation?
- ⊙ Realistically, what is the worst that can happen and how would that affect my life?
- ⊙ How will this seem to me in a week's time/month's time/year's time?
- ⊙ Having considered the above, what is the most helpful thing I can do next?

EXAMPLES OF MINDFULNESS SKILLS

- ⊙ avoiding stimulants, including caffeine;
- ⊙ occupying and balancing your attention with music and using a walkman; doing something active, such as physical exercise, to help take your mind off your feelings;
- ⊙ relaxation, awareness and mindfulness exercises, meditation;
- ⊙ reminding yourself of your positive goal by using a cue card. Speaking to someone, getting help and support, planning a number of steps and taking them one at a time.

REFERENCES

Beck, A.T., Freeman, A. *et al.* (1990) Borderline personality disorder. In *Cognitive Therapy of Personality Disorders* (pp. 176–207). London: Guilford Press.

Linehan, M.M. (1993). *Skills Training Manual for Treating Borderline Personality Disorder*. New York: Guilford Press.

Paris, J. (1994). *Borderline Personality Disorder. A Multi-dimensional Approach*. Washington, DC: American Psychiatric Association.

Ryle, A. (1995). *Cognitive Analytic Therapy. Developments in Theory and Practice.* Chichester: Wiley.

Thich Nhat Hanh (1991). *Peace is Every Step. The Path of Mindfulness in Everyday Life.* London: Bantam Books.

USEFUL READING

Allica, G. (1998). *Meditation is Easy.* Harmondsworth: Penguin.

Braza, J. (1998). *Moment by Moment. The Art and Practice of Mindfulness.* Boston, Mass.: Eden Grove.

Carrington, P. (1999). *The Power of Letting Go. A Practical Approach to Releasing the Pressures in Your Life.* Shaftesbury, Dorset: Element.

Goleman, D. (1996). *Emotional Intelligence.* London: Bloomsbury.

Harrison, E. (1993). *Teach Yourself to Meditate. Over 20 Simple Exercises for Peace, Health and Clarity of Mind.* London: Piatkus.

Jeffers, S. (1991) *Feel the Fear and Do It Anyway.* London: Century.

Jeffers, S. (1998). *Feel the Fear and Beyond.* London: Century Ryder.

Kabat-Zinn, J. (1990). *Full Catastrophe Living: The Program of the Stress Reduction Clinic at the University of Massachusetts Medical Center.* New York: Dell Publishing.

Wilde McCormick, E. (1990). *Change for the Better. A Life-changing Self-help Psychotherapy Programme.* London: Unwin.

Review of Chapter 6

Please circle your answer to each of the following:

How much of the chapter did you read?

0%   25%   50%   75%   100%

Overall, was it

Very helpful   Helpful   Not relevant to me   Don't know   Unhelpful

Did you/your client complete Exercise 6.1?

Yes   No

Was it

Very helpful   Helpful   Don't know   Unhelpful

Did you/your client complete Exercise 6.2?

Yes   No

Was it

Very helpful   Helpful   Don't know   Unhelpful

Did you/your client complete Exercise 6.3?

Yes   No

Was it

Very helpful   Helpful   Don't know   Unhelpful

Did you/your client complete Exercise 6.4?

Yes   No

Was it

Very helpful   Helpful   Don't know   Unhelpful

Did you/your client complete Exercise 6.5?

Yes   No

Was it

Very helpful   Helpful   Don't know   Unhelpful

Did you/your client complete Exercise 6.6?

Yes   No

Was it

Very helpful   Helpful   Don't know   Unhelpful

Did you/your client complete Exercise 6.7?

Yes   No

Was it

Very helpful   Helpful   Don't know   Unhelpful

Did you/your client complete Exercise 6.8?

Yes   No

Was it

Very helpful   Helpful   Don't know   Unhelpful

Did you/your client complete Exercise 6.9?

Yes   No

Was it

Very helpful   Helpful   Don't know   Unhelpful

Did you/your client complete Exercise 6.10?

Yes   No

Was it

Very helpful   Helpful   Don't know   Unhelpful

Did you/your client complete Exercise 6.11?

Yes   No

Was it

Very helpful   Helpful   Don't know   Unhelpful

Did you/your client complete Exercise 6.12?

Yes   No

Was it

Very helpful   Helpful   Don't know   Unhelpful

Comments

Investigating and modifying thinking habits and beliefs

Cognitive therapy is now a major field within psychotherapy and mental health. The knowledge that our thoughts play an important role in shaping our mental and emotional life has been around a long time. In order to manage your moods better, you need to become aware of your thoughts and how they influence your emotions, as well as how your emotions change the way you think. Butler and Hope (1995) illustrate how thoughts and feelings interact to produce depression or anxiety.

**E
X
E   7.1
R
C
I
S
E**

Write down on the left all the feelings you have when you are depressed. Put them in the sequence they occur. For example, maybe it begins with you feeling fed up, escalates to miserable, etc. Use your own words.

Now write down on the right the kind of thoughts you have when you are depressed: 'Nobody cares about me', 'I'm a bad person', 'I hate myself'. Again put them in the order you think they happen.

Using arrows, see if you can link the two lists to describe your own personal cycle of depression. (This describes what happens in a downward spiral. You can also do it in a vicious circle – whichever seems to most reflect your experience.)

Do you ever have a problem with anxiety or anger? If so you could repeat the exercise for those emotions.

THINKING PATTERNS WHICH ARE LIKELY TO CONTRIBUTE TO YOUR PROBLEMS

We are all prone at times to 'distorted thinking', but when we are either under excess stress or depressed these distortions become more exaggerated. The following patterns have been identified as contributing to and maintaining a wide range of mental health problems. All of them are relevant to the problems of people with borderline problems.

I have used asterisks to highlight how central I think they may be to your problems: * plays a role, ** plays a major role, *** is core to your problems. Recognising them and catching yourself doing them will help enormously.

***Black-or-white/all-or-nothing thinking

Thinking in absolutes, as either black or white, good or bad, with no middle ground. You may trust others completely or not at all. You may condemn yourself completely as a person on the basis of a single event.

**Catastrophizing

This is when you tend to magnify and exaggerate the importance of events and how awful or unpleasant they will be, overestimating the chances of disaster; whatever can go wrong will go wrong – for example, telling yourself you will never cope if someone leaves you. You are likely to do this when you are in crisis.

***Exaggerating and over-generalising

Taking one example and making general conclusions as if that were the case all the time, or with everyone. You are likely to do this in the areas where you are hypersensitive – trust, rejection, being let down. Words to watch out for are:

- *always*: 'people always sh.. on me'
- *never*: 'you never show me you care'
- *nobody*: 'nobody cares whether I live or die'

***Mind-reading/jumping to conclusions

Making assumptions about how others are thinking, or their motives for their behaviour. You are likely to do this when you are mistrustful or 'paranoid'. Making negative interpretations even though there are no definite facts. Predicting the future.

***Taking things personally

Taking responsibility and blame for anything unpleasant even if it has little or nothing to do with you. Assuming actions or comments are directed at you when they aren't necessarily. For example, when someone makes a general comment you interpret this as them having a dig at you. Dwelling on feelings of being injured and how someone else is 'out to get you'.

***Negative focus/discounting the positive

Focusing on the negative, ignoring or misinterpreting positive aspects of a situation. You may focus on your weaknesses and forget your strengths, looking on the dark side. You are certainly likely to do this when you are feeling depressed. Anyone who is depressed attends selectively; that is, they notice, think about, brood over negative things and omit to notice, remember or focus on positives.

*Living by fixed rules/'judging mind'

Having fixed rules and unrealistic expectations, regularly using the words 'should', 'ought', 'must' and 'can't'. For example, 'I shouldn't be like this . . . I ought to be able to cope.' This leads to you invalidating your feelings, and contributes to you feeling guilty and disappointed.

***Emotional reasoning

Assuming that because you feel or think something that is how it really is. Convincing yourself of a position or perspective on something on the basis of your feelings. Believing your feelings are accurate when they aren't. This is a biggie!

You can see how some of these feed into others. For example, when you feel let down by someone and end up feeling no one cares about you, you may be generalising, discounting positives, black-and-white thinking and emotional reasoning!

1 Look through the list and write examples of each from your own thinking at times. You may not think like that all the time. (Clue: consider your bad states and identify how you think at those times.)

2 Now go through the list and try and define the opposite style of thinking. For example, the opposite of living by fixed rules/judging mind is being flexible and tolerant. Then look at your examples and think of an opposite for each.

Home study **Mood and thoughts diary**

It will be helpful to keep a 'thought' diary whenever you notice a problem in your mood or behaviour. You can then check your thought patterns against this list and discuss it in sessions. Here's a simple format to use:

Day and date	Event/situation (e.g. someone who promised to phone me didn't)	Feelings (hurt and angry)	Thoughts ('they don't care about me' 'I can't trust them' 'You can't trust anyone')

You may not find it easy to change your thought habits, but it is probably essential that you do in order to feel happier and to manage your life better. There are many self-help books available which describe how you can do this, such as those by Burns (1980, 1990) or Greenburger and Padesky (1995) (see Chapter 8). The first step is to accept that the way you interpret experience is subjective and therefore inevitably subject to bias. This is true for us all, but few of us like to admit it! We all want to think that our view is right. Accepting that our views and opinions are just that and subject to bias is a big step. Then you can begin to be more detached from your emotions rather than controlled by them. With practice, you can question your responses and assumptions in a way which will benefit you.

RE-EVALUATING YOUR THOUGHTS AND BELIEFS

Here are some useful questions to ask when reviewing your thought diary:

- What are the consequences of thinking this way?
- What other points of view are there? What would my best friend say? How would someone else think about this?
- Am I being misled by how I feel inside rather than focusing on the facts? If I was in a different mood would I think differently? How?
- Am I doing any of the above thought patterns (e.g. black-and-white thinking, ignoring the positives?) Am I basing my judgement on one isolated incident?
- Has there been a time I thought this and it turned out not to be true?
- What is the evidence in support of my thought or belief? What is the evidence against it?
- How else could I think about it?

HOLDING A DIFFERENT VIEWPOINT

Here are some examples of common negative thoughts and alternative thoughts which can help you challenge them. These are not for you to rehearse or copy, but ideas for you to use in reviewing how you can begin to change. This may seem simplistic when your emotions are very intense, but with consistent practice you really can change thought habits. You weren't born with them were you ? You learnt them and you can unlearn them.

Negative thought	Challenge
I can't stand it.	I can stand it. It's difficult, but I can put up with it. It will help me to cope better if I practise.
I am not good enough.	I'm not perfect. Like everyone I'm good at some things and bad at others.
What's the point in trying?	If I don't try, I won't know. Trying may mean I gain some confidence. Not trying will mean I definitely won't.
What if I make a mistake? It would be awful.	Everybody makes mistakes. That's the way we learn.
If people knew the real me they wouldn't like me.	There are things about me that are likeable and things that aren't – just like everyone else.
Nobody likes me.	People can like me. I have had better relationships in the past and will in the future.
Everybody else is happier than me.	Actually this is unlikely to be true. I don't tell everyone my problems. I can't know that others don't have problems too.
I'm no good at relationships. I should keep away from people.	I need to work at getting on better with people. No one can live without relationships.
I'm hopeless at everything. I'll never sort my problems out.	Just take one step at a time. If I do this I can tackle my problems little by little.

EXERCISE **7.4** *Home study*

Continue to keep a thought diary and record a challenging thought you tried to use. If you want to write down triggers put them in the day and date column.

Day and date	Thoughts	How I challenged them

COGNITIVE SCHEMAS

Schemas are core beliefs which are shaped by and in turn shape our experience of the world. Examining these can be a useful aid to understanding problems which are resistant to change. Schemas are the result of our early experience and the way we have made sense of our experience.

You may have a persistent belief and feeling that:

⊙ there is something wrong with you, that you are unlovable (defectiveness schema) or don't fit in (social isolation schema);
⊙ others will abuse you or can't be trusted (mistrust/abuse schema);
⊙ others will leave you and find this devastating and unbearable (abandonment schema). You may:
⊙ feel you will never get the love you need (emotional deprivation schema) and
⊙ try to maintain relationships by pleasing others (subjugation schema) or get angry when you don't get your own way (entitlement schema) or
⊙ find it difficult to work towards long-term goals (insufficient self-control).

Once we have these core beliefs they shape the way we perceive everything. If we experience something which could challenge them, we may not notice it, we may discount it (telling ourselves it's an exception), or distort our perception or interpretation of it.

EXERCISE 7.5

Schema questionnaire (Young and Brown, 1990)

Complete the following questionnaire and see which schemas you have.

Listed below are statements that a person might use to describe himself or herself. Please read each statement and decide how well it describes you. When you are not sure, base your answer on what you emotionally feel, not on what you think to be true. Choose the highest rating from 1 to 6 that describes you and write the number in the space before the statement.

Rating scale:
1 = completely untrue of me
2 = mostly untrue of me
3 = slightly more true than untrue
4 = moderately true of me
5 = mostly true of me
6 = describes me perfectly

1   Most of the time I haven't had someone to nurture me, share him/herself with me, or care deeply about everything that happens to me.

2   In general people have not been there to give me warmth, holding and affection.

3   For much of my life, I haven't felt that I am special to someone.

4   For the most part I have not had someone who really listens to me, understands me or is tuned into my true needs and feelings.
[*ed]

5   I have rarely had a strong person to give me sound advice or direction when I'm not sure what to do.

6   I find myself clinging to people I'm close to because I'm afraid they'll leave me.

7   I need other people so much that I worry about losing them.

8   I worry that people I feel close to will leave me or abandon me.

9   When I feel someone I care for pulling away from me, I get desperate.

10   Sometimes I am so worried about people leaving me that I drive them away.
[*ab]

11   I feel that people will take advantage of me.

12   I feel that I cannot let my guard down in the presence of other people, or else they will intentionally hurt me.

13   It is only a matter of time before someone betrays me.

14   I am quite suspicious of other people's motives.

15   I'm usually on the look out for people's ulterior motives.
[*ma]

16   I don't fit in.

17   I'm fundamentally different from other people.

18   I don't belong; I'm a loner.

19   I feel alienated from other people.

20   I always feel on the outside of groups.
[*si]

21   No man/woman I desire could love me once he/she saw my defects.

22   No one I desire would want to stay close to me if he/she knew the real me.

23   I'm unworthy of the love, attention and respect of others.

24   I feel that I'm unlovable.

25   I am too unacceptable in very basic ways to reveal myself to other people.
[*ds]

26   Almost nothing I do at work (or college) is as good as other people can do.

27   I'm incompetent when it comes to achievement.

28   Most other people are more capable than I am in areas of work and achievement.

29   I'm not as talented as most people are at their work.

30   I'm not as intelligent as most people when it comes to work.
[*fa]

31   I do not feel capable of getting by on my own in everyday life.

32   I think of myself as a dependent person when it comes to everyday functioning.

33   I lack common sense.

34   My judgement cannot be relied upon in everyday situations.

35   I don't feel confident about my ability to solve everyday problems that come up.
[*di]

36   I can't seem to escape the feeling that something bad is about to happen to me.

37   I feel that a disaster (natural, criminal, financial or medical) could strike at any moment.

38   I worry about being attacked.

39   I worry that I'll lose all my money and become destitute.

40   I worry that I'm developing a serious illness, even though nothing serious has been diagnosed by a doctor.
[*vh]

41   I have not been able to separate myself from my parent(s) the way other people my age seem to.

42   My parent(s) and I tend to be over-involved in each other's lives and problems.

43   It is very difficult for my parents and me to keep intimate details from each other, without feeling betrayed or guilty.

44   I often feel as if my parent(s) are living through me – I don't have a life of my own.

45   I often feel that I do not have a separate identity from my parents or partner.
[*em]

46   I think if I do what I want, I'm only asking for trouble.

47   I feel that I have no choice but to give in to other people's wishes or else they will retaliate or reject me in some way.

48   In relationships, I let the other person have the upper hand.

49   I've always let others make choices for me, so I really don't know what I want for myself.

50   I have a lot of trouble demanding that my rights be respected and that my feelings be taken into account. [*sb]

51   I'm the one who usually ends up taking care of the people I'm close to.

52   I am a good person because I think of others more than of myself.

53   I'm so busy doing things for the people I care about that I have little time for myself.

54   I've always been the one who listens to everyone else's problems.

55   Other people see me as doing too much for others and not enough for myself. [*ss]

56   I am too self-conscious to show positive feelings to others (e.g. affection, showing I care).

57   I find it embarrassing to express my feelings to others.

58   I find it hard to be warm and spontaneous.

59   I control myself so much that people think I am unemotional.

60   People see me as uptight emotionally. [*ei]

61   I must be the best at most of what I do; I can't accept second best.

62   I try to do my best; I can't settle for good enough.

63   I must meet all my responsibilities.

64   I feel there is constant pressure for me to achieve and get things done.

65   I can't let myself off the hook easily or make excuses for my mistakes. [*us]

66   I have a lot of trouble accepting no for an answer when I want something from other people.

67   I'm special and shouldn't have to accept many of the restrictions placed on other people.

68   I hate to be constrained or kept from doing what I want.

69   I feel that I shouldn't have to follow the normal rules and conventions other people do.

70   I feel that what I have to offer is of greater value than the contributions of others.
[*et]

71   I can't seem to discipline myself to complete routine or boring tasks.

72   If I can't reach a goal, I become easily frustrated and give up.

73   I have a very difficult time sacrificing immediate gratification to achieve a long-range goal.

74   I can't force myself to do things I don't enjoy, even when I know it's for my own good.

75   I have rarely been able to stick to my own resolutions.
[*is]

* = Abbreviations in scoring chart which follows.

Now circle all scores of 5 or 6. How many of these do you have in each section? Put a cross on this grid under *the number of items in each section which you scored 5 or 6*. This will be between 0 and 5. Then write in your total score (i.e. how many you scored 5 or 6 on – the score will be between 0 and 75) and put a cross in the column approximately where your score would be.

How many in each section scored 5 or 6?

	0	1 (20%)	2 (40%)	3 (60%)	4 (80%)	5 (100%)
ed – emotional deprivation (1–5)						
ab – abandonment (6–10)						
ma – mistrust/abuse (11–15)						
si – social isolation (16–20)						
ds – defectiveness (21–25)						
fa – failure (26–30)						
di – dependency (31–35)						
vh – vulnerability to harm (36–40)						
em – enmeshment or undeveloped self (41–45)						
sb – subjugation (46–50)						
ss – self-sacrifice (51–55)						
el – emotional inhibition (56–60)						
us – unrelenting standards (61–65)						
et – entitlement (66–70)						
is – insufficient self-control (71–75)						

| Total score | 0 | 15 | 30 | 45 | 60 | 75 |

Discuss in sessions which of these are the biggest problem for you. This will help you make sense of the problems we identified were part of your diagnosis. For example, if you have paranoid thoughts about others, which schema do you think is operating? Another way of tapping schemas is to discuss or note down your childhood experiences. Then think about the sense you made of them at the time; the conclusions you came to about yourself, about others and about the world.

E
X
E
R
C
I
S
E

7.6 Try this exercise. Compare what you say to the schemas above.

I am . . .

Other people always . . .

I think the world/life . . .

7.7 *Home study*

Whenever you have a very powerful emotional state a schema has been triggered. Continue the *emotions diary and for every record think about which schema has been triggered, if any, and make a note of this on the diary.*

Understanding and identifying your schemas is very important if you are going to successfully manage your life. *Reinventing Your Life* by Young and Klosko (1993) is a very helpful guide to identifying and changing schemas or 'life traps'. There are chapters on each of the most common schema. It is probably the most important book for you to read in addition to your manual.

People develop a range of ways of dealing with schemas. For example they may do what they can in order to avoid triggering the painful feelings associated with them (*schema avoidance*). So if you have an abandonment schema you will probably cling to people. You may try really hard to get people to like you (e.g. do a lot for others or buy people things). You may at times go to extreme lengths to try and stop people abandoning you, such as trying to take your life.

When our beliefs are very ingrained we often behave in ways which confirm our beliefs. Schema are very powerful influences in our lives; they are familiar to us. This can be described as a self-fulfilling prophecy and these patterns will maintain a schema (*schema maintenance*). A lot of things people with borderline problems do will actually maintain the schema. For example, getting angry with others or harming yourself will increase the risk of being rejected by others and thereby reinforce your fear of abandonment schema and/or your belief that you are bad (defectiveness schema) or different from others (social isolation schema).

We can also try to make up for or 'compensate' for them. For example, if you hate yourself you may try hard to make yourself feel better (e.g. try to be thin). This is known as *schema compensation*. Expecting people to meet your needs all the time is a way of compensating for feeling deprived or let down.

EXERCISE 7.8 Schema avoidance, maintenance and compensation

In your session, write down the schemas you have identified as a problem for you. Taking one at a time, think about any way that you try to avoid triggering the schema, habit patterns that may maintain it, and finally any way you try and compensate for it.

Schema:

How does it get reinforced?	How do I avoid it?	How do I try and make up for it?

You can repeat this with another schema

You probably have a number of schemas which appear to contradict each other and may switch quickly between them. It may seem as if you have only two choices; that is, to hate others and be angry with them or to blame and hate yourself. Some people will enact both according to which is most strongly triggered (e.g. getting violently angry with others at times and violent to themselves at others times). Other people will avoid one (e.g. blame of and anger with others) so take it out on themselves (e.g. self-harm instead of getting angry with someone else). When you have identified these take some time to work through ways in which you might try and change, both by modifying your beliefs and changing your behaviour. If you have a dependence or incompetence schema this will be a difficult and slow process. You may have to consider the pros and cons of change as described in Chapter 5.

EXERCISE 7.9 **Reviewing the evidence for your beliefs**

Take a schema which is a problem for you (e.g. that you are unlovable or people always let you down). Write it down here:

Write down all the evidence that you think *supports* the belief.

Are there any ways you can reframe these? For example, your belief may be that you are worthless and support of this may be that you have done bad things. You could re-evaluate this and tell yourself that everyone does good and bad things; having done bad things does not mean you are worthless. You have also done good things.

What would be a new alternative belief?

Then write a list of evidence that challenges your old belief and supports the new belief.

Write this list on cards for use at home. Recite the re-evaluation and alternative evidence to help change or weaken one negative core belief.

E
X **7.10** *Home study*
E
R Keep a diary of everything which supports the new belief.
C
I
S
E

Changing core beliefs is not easy, but is possible with determination and continuous effort. This is a process you will need to continue throughout the programme.

REFERENCES

Butler, G. and Hope, T. (1995). *The Mental Fitness Guide: Managing your Mind*. Oxford: Oxford University Press.

Burns, D. (1980). *Feeling Good: The New Mood Therapy*. New York: William Morrow.

Burns, D. (2000). *The Feeling Good Handbook: Using the New Mood Therapy in Everyday Life*. London: Penguin.

**Greenberger, D. and Padesky, C. (1995). *Mind Over Mood: A Cognitive Therapy Treatment Manual for Clients*. New York: Guilford Press.

Young, J.E. and Brown, G. (1990). *The Schema Questionnaire*. New York: Cognitive Therapy Centre of New York.

**Young, J.E. and Klosko, J.S. (1993). *Reinventing Your Life. How to Break Free from Negative Life Patterns and Feel Good Again*. New York: Plume Books.

(**Highly recommended)

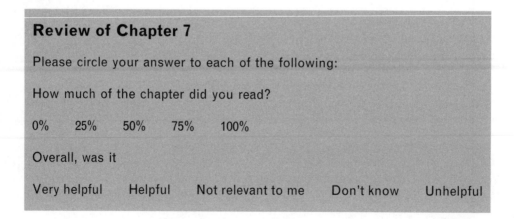

Review of Chapter 7

Please circle your answer to each of the following:

How much of the chapter did you read?

0%   25%   50%   75%   100%

Overall, was it

Very helpful   Helpful   Not relevant to me   Don't know   Unhelpful

Did you/your client complete Exercise 7.1?

Yes   No

Was it

Very helpful   Helpful   Don't know   Unhelpful

Did you/your client complete Exercise 7.2?

Yes   No

Was it

Very helpful   Helpful   Don't know   Unhelpful

Did you/your client complete Exercise 7.3?

Yes   No

Was it

Very helpful   Helpful   Don't know   Unhelpful

Did you/your client complete Exercise 7.4?

Yes   No

Was it

Very helpful   Helpful   Don't know   Unhelpful

Did you/your client complete Exercise 7.5?

Yes   No

Was it

Very helpful   Helpful   Don't know   Unhelpful

Did you/your client complete Exercise 7.6?

Yes   No

Was it

Very helpful   Helpful   Don't know   Unhelpful

Did you/your client complete Exercise 7.7?

Yes   No

Was it

Very helpful   Helpful   Don't know   Unhelpful

Did you/your client complete Exercise 7.8?

Yes   No

Was it

Very helpful   Helpful   Don't know   Unhelpful

Did you/your client complete Exercise 7.9?

Yes   No

Was it

Very helpful   Helpful   Don't know   Unhelpful

Did you/your client complete Exercise 7.10?

Yes   No

Was it

Very helpful   Helpful   Don't know   Unhelpful

Comments

PART 2

Tackling the problems

Overcoming depression and managing difficult mood states

All people with borderline problems suffer with mood shifts (i.e. intense sudden changes in mood, usually lasting a few hours). Many also suffer with periods (days, weeks or months) of depression. Suicidal feelings can happen in extreme, sudden mood states (e.g. when you feel rejected or abandoned), or when you are severely depressed for a long time. *Alcohol* is a depressant. If you are drinking heavily this will certainly contribute to you being depressed. Revisit Chapter 5 and consider reducing your alcohol intake. Whilst *medication* may have little to offer you with other problems (without side effects), it is almost certainly possible for your mood to be improved with medication, particularly if you have biological features of depression. These include sleep disturbance, appetite disturbance and decreased physical activity.

Butler and Hope (1995) suggest three ways of reducing depression:

⊙ work on your activities;
⊙ work on your thoughts;
⊙ work on your support systems.

Let's look at each in turn.

ACTIVITY

When we are depressed we tend to slow down because we have less enthusiasm and motivation. People who are more active (i.e. engage in activities which direct their attention outwards and/or physical exercise) are less likely to be depressed. Our thoughts, activity and mood interact:

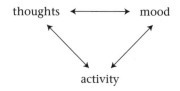

In order to assess whether this is an area which you can make beneficial changes in, it's helpful to keep an activity diary.

E
X   Can you think of examples from your own experience of how
E   behaviour influences your emotions. For example, doing some
R   exercise tends to make you feel energetic while sitting around
C   not doing much can make you feel lethargic.
I
S
E

E
X **8.2** Have a look at the example given on the next page. What can
E   you discover from this diary about the person's activity and
R   mood?
C
I
S
E

What else could they have done that might have given them more mastery or pleasure?

What they did and when	Mastery (0–10)	Pleasure (0–10)
8 get up	2	0
8.05–8.15 have a drink	1	1
8.15–9.00 watch TV	0	1
9.00–9.15 have breakfast	1	1
9.15–9.30 washed my hair	3 I'd wanted to do it for a few days	3 It was nice to have clean hair

9.35 got dressed	2	1
9.40 tidy up	4 This took a lot of effort	2 I felt better seeing the house tidy

10.00 go to the shops	2	1
11.00 visited a friend	4	6
12.15 walked home	3	3 I enjoyed the walk
1.00 watched TV	0	1

E X E R C I S E **8.3** *Home study*

Keep a diary like this for a week so that you can discuss it in sessions. It's very simple. Just write down *everything* you do and for how long. (You will need your own paper and notebook.)

This will give a clear picture of the pattern of your day and how long you spend doing various things. Try as far as possible to complete the diary as you go along; don't leave it till the end of the day (or the next week!), as it won't be accurate. This may seem tedious, but it will be very useful to then review.

At the end of each day go through the list and give each activity a score for mastery (sense of achievement) and a score for pleasure (enjoyment). If what you did was difficult and took effort then recognise this with the mastery score.

Here's a guideline for scoring:

0 – no mastery or pleasure	1 – a little	3 – some
6 – quite a bit	8 – a lot	10 – loads!

Complete your diary for a week and then discuss how much mastery and pleasure you get from the ways you have spent time.

EXERCISE 8.4

What gives you a sense of pleasure and mastery?

Do you spend long periods of time doing things that don't give you much pleasure or mastery?

Are there times of the day when this is consistently low?

Are there things you have stopped doing that you used to enjoy? What are they?

If you were less depressed, how would you spend your time differently?

What's your daily routine like? Do you have one?

Generally, the sooner you get up and dressed the less likely you are to feel depressed.

See if you can generate your own ideas about how you might increase your sense of mastery and pleasure. What can you plan to do more of? – big events like visiting people or small things like having a bath, washing your hair.

When you set goals try and take things in small steps so that you can achieve them successfully. Make your goals as specific as possible. A goal like 'mix more socially' is rather vague and will be difficult for you to act on.

Antidotes to depression

Some things which are very difficult to do when you are depressed are a positive antidote and, if you can do them regularly, will lift your mood. These include:

⊙ laughter
⊙ singing
⊙ inspiration (from poetry, art, spiritual faith)
⊙ exercise

In India laughter is considered so therapeutic that there are clubs where people meet to make each other laugh (pulling funny faces at each other, telling jokes). When you're depressed it is very hard to laugh or sing. But if you can, it really helps to lighten your mood.

Which television programmes do you find most funny? Try and watch them every week. Which music is most likely to get you singing? (Something like the Beatles, Simon and Garfunkel, Frank Sinatra, Abba.) It needs to be something cheerful, and music you know well so it is less of an effort.

EXERCISE **8.5** *Home study*

Put some music on that you know the words to. Try and sing along. If you can get into it, try and sing at full volume. If this is embarrassing turn the volume up! Try and do this everyday. Tune into a radio station that plays your old favourites and try and sing along. What gives you inspiration (uplifts you, gives you hope and joy)?

If nothing does, maybe this is something you could explore. Try reading some poetry. Start with an anthology of popular poems. This may seem sentimental, but it will help you to cultivate other states of mind and build the skills you need to overcome depression.

Physical activity is one of the best antidotes to depression. Research trials show that it can be as effective at tackling depression as medication. Those who exercised actually maintained their improved mood better in the long run because they had learnt to do something differently. And it's good for you physically and can help you mix more.

EXERCISE **8.6**

What physical activity do you most enjoy?

Would you like to do something that you could do at any time (e.g. jogging or cycling), or would you rather do something with others such as badminton?

What could you do regularly that you could keep up?

Is there someone you could do it with? (This is a mixed blessing. If the other person gives up, are you willing to keep at it?)

THOUGHTS

You are not your emotions

If you are able to know, witness, describe your emotions then you cannot be them. That part of you which is not the emotion (who is aware, reflecting) is that part of you which has choices. Getting a handle on your life will depend on how much you can understand this and then apply this understanding in developing detachment from your emotions. Practising mindfulness regularly will help you to feel more at peace with whatever emotional state you are in, with yourself.

When your mood is low you can use the strategies we covered in Chapter 6 to begin to change the way you think. These strategies work, but only if you use them regularly. A shorthand way or reminding yourself what you need to do is:

⦾ *Stop*. Pause and reflect. Name the emotion you are experiencing. Notice your thoughts.
⦾ *Think* about what's happening – consider the thinking habits contributing to the way you feel and which schema have been triggered. What options you have.
⦾ *Plan* what you are going to do. Discuss what is likely to work for you and write down some options.

Patiently enduring *and* cultivating opposite states of mind

Some mood states just have to be endured. Endurance is not a quality which is likely to come easily to you. You probably have strong feelings of wanting, yearning, craving ('You must help me') and strong feelings of aversion ('I can't stand . . .', 'I hate . . .'). Remember from Chapter 6 that all emotional states change, so if you can endure them long enough you can come out the other side. Enduring doesn't mean being a helpless, powerless victim. It means patiently bearing with something until it passes. You may feel something (let's say abandoned and desperately alone) and be unable to take away this feeling. But you have many choices about how you manage that feeling.

One choice you can make is to decide to cultivate a different state to the one you are feeling. For example, if you feel resentful and angry you can try to do something generous – maybe buy someone a bunch of flowers, write them a note saying what you appreciate about them. If you can't manage it, it doesn't have to be the same person you feel angry with or resentful of. The purpose is to cultivate a contrasting state of mind primarily for your benefit. This is similar to the techniques used in some therapy programmes known as 'acting as if'. So if you feel thick, stupid, can't do anything, you choose to act as if you are not stupid, you are competent and the thing is worth doing. If you feel hopeless and despairing and want to stay in bed all day, you act as if you are feeling differently by getting up and being productive. The aim here is to separate your behaviour from your feelings. Changing your behaviour is one way of starting to change your feelings.

EXERCISE **8.7**

You may believe that your emotions are so intense at times that you have no choices. Let's take a look at that belief. Think of the last time you felt abandoned. How did you manage that feeling?

Think of other times you have felt like that. Were there times you handled it better and other times you handled it less well? What made the difference?

How and when did your choices come into play?

EXERCISE **8.8** Think of all the possible things you could do when you feel abandoned and desperately lonely. Think of as many as you can.

Now put them in order of unwise to wise (see Chapter 6). Why have you put them in that order? Why are some wise and others unwise?

SUPPORT

In an important research study of depression in women, Brown and Harris (1978) examined many aspects of women's lives. They found that women who had someone they trusted and confided in were the least likely to become depressed. Ideally we need a number of people we can get support from – not just one. This can put a lot of strain on that relationship and leave you vulnerable if you the lose the friendship. Do you feel able to confide in anyone about your problems? If not, why not? See Chapter 12 on building better relationships.

THE VOID OR PIT AND SUICIDAL FEELINGS

One of the most difficult states for people with borderline problems is an aching sense of emptiness, a void. It can feel totally engulfing – like a bottomless pit you are unable to get out of. Utter despair.

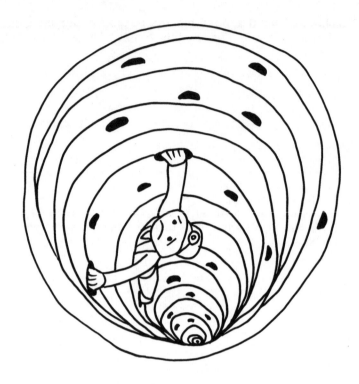

This state is described in Chapter 12 as a 'frozen need'. It is usually triggered when you feel abandoned or rejected. It may include overwhelming grief (uncontrollable sobbing), 'existential' panic and fear (what is described in children as separation anxiety). It usually comes from very early experiences of loss or neglect, when you were a baby or infant. This state is very difficult to reason yourself out of because it's like having a record replayed which was installed when you had no reasoning; just primitive needs and responses.

Does this sound familiar to you? If so what triggers it and what tends to happen? You will need to have a plan of how to deal with it, with a range of options (the same thing won't work all the time). The urge will be to find comfort and care from someone else (like you will die without it). If the 'adult' part of you feels unable to ask for this, you may do things to elicit it like self-harm or threaten suicide. You may feel unable to trust anyone or feel so guilty that you punish yourself or want to end your life.

Managing these feelings requires the use of all the skills we have covered in Chapters 6, 7 and in this one. Dealing with very severe difficult mind states like suicidal feelings and rage requires that you intervene earlier in the cycle. Although you may have relatively sudden mood swings, you will not be OK one minute then suicidal the next. Something will happen to upset you. Maybe you have been let down by someone or feel rejected. Then you will brood on this, thinking such thoughts as 'Nobody cares about me', 'I can't trust anyone'. This can then quickly spiral into 'What's the point in living', and maybe a fantasy that if you are completely helpless and needing care someone will care for you. You can see the steps involved, the schema of abandonment and mistrust, the black-and-white, over-generalising thinking (Chapter 7), the search for perfect care (Chapter 12).

When you become more skilled at tackling each of these, which will only happen with effort and practice, then you will be able to manage suicidal states better. You will be able to know that the anguish is something that will pass, to reflect on the fact that you have felt that way before and it does pass. It is a cliché, but also a very profound truth and a great comfort. What it takes is:

⊙ awareness ('I am not this emotion'),
⊙ understanding ('Emotions change, come and go'), and
⊙ patience ('I can handle it, occupy myself until I feel better').

In Chapter 6 we also looked at crises and suggested that you have a plan for managing these times with your options written down. Then when you 'lose it' and can't think straight you can get out your crisis card with suggestions about what you can do. Keep it somewhere close – your handbag or bedroom cabinet. Maybe two copies will be useful. This should include phoning Samaritans or the mental health service. Try and use both; that way you have more options.

E
X 8.9 *Home study*
E
R
C
I
S
E

Quick ways of releasing difficult states
If you practise regularly these work.

Quick way of releasing tension
Scan your body for tension. Where you can feel it (jaw, teeth, eyes, hands)? Release the muscles and breathe into that part of your body, saying to yourself 'release'.

Quick ways of releasing anxiety
Breathe in 'iiiiiiiiiiiiiiiiiiiinn . . .' Breathe out 'ouuuuuuuuuuut . . .'
'Calm . . . .'

E X E R C I S E **8.10** Try a half smile (closing your eyes helps concentration). Spend the rest of this week practising when your mood is low.

REFERENCES AND FURTHER READING

Brown, G.W. and Harris, T.W. (1978). *Social Origins of Depression. A Study of Psychiatric Disorder in Women*. London: Tavistock Publications.

Butler, G. and Hope, T. (1995). *Manage Your Mind: The Mental Fitness Guide*. Oxford: Oxford University Press.

Gilbert, P. (1997). *Overcoming Depression. A Self-help Guide Using Cognitive-behavioural Techniques*. London: Robinson.

Greenberger, D. and Padesky, C. (1995). *Mind over Mood: A Cognitive Therapy Treatment Manual for Clients*. New York: Guilford Press.

Holmes, R. and Holmes, J. (1993). *The Good Mood Guide*. London: JM Dent.

Scott, J. (2001). *Overcoming Mood Swings*. London: Constable & Robinson.

Thayer, R.E. (1996). *The Origin of Everyday Moods. Managing Energy, Tension and Stress*. Oxford: Oxford University Press.

Review of Chapter 8

Please circle your answer to each of the following:

How much of the chapter did you read?

0%   25%   50%   75%   100%

Overall, was it

Very helpful   Helpful   Not relevant to me   Don't know   Unhelpful

Did you/your client complete Exercise 8.1?

Yes   No

Was it

Very helpful   Helpful   Don't know   Unhelpful

Did you/your client complete Exercise 8.2?

Yes   No

Was it

Very helpful   Helpful   Don't know   Unhelpful

Did you/your client complete Exercise 8.3?

Yes   No

Was it

Very helpful   Helpful   Don't know   Unhelpful

Did you/your client complete Exercise 8.4?

Yes   No

Was it

Very helpful   Helpful   Don't know   Unhelpful

Did you/your client complete Exercise 8.5?

Yes   No

Was it

Very helpful   Helpful   Don't know   Unhelpful

Did you/your client complete Exercise 8.6?

Yes   No

Was it

Very helpful   Helpful   Don't know   Unhelpful

Did you/your client complete Exercise 8.7?

Yes   No

Was it

Very helpful   Helpful   Don't know   Unhelpful

Did you/your client complete Exercise 8.8?

Yes   No

Was it

Very helpful   Helpful   Don't know   Unhelpful

Did you/your client complete Exercise 8.9?

Yes   No

Was it

Very helpful   Helpful   Don't know   Unhelpful

Did you/your client complete Exercise 8.10?

Yes   No

Was it

Very helpful   Helpful   Don't know   Unhelpful

Comments

Tackling childhood abuse

If you have experienced any kind of abuse as a child this will not be an easy area to tackle. It is important for you to discuss your feelings about this before working on the issues this chapter raises. If you are worried about difficult feelings and memories from your childhood you need to make a plan of how you can manage these feelings.

There are many forms of child abuse. Not all people who've been abused realise this because they may have grown up thinking such behaviour was normal or that in some way they deserved it. It is important for you to identify what abuse or neglect you have experienced. Then consider how this has affected you – how you feel about yourself and patterns in your relationships with others (see Chapters 11 and 12). Forms of abuse are:

⊙ *Emotional* – ridicule, humiliation, verbal abuse (being called stupid, fat, clumsy, ugly), cruelty, exploiting, depriving, or threatening a child (such as threatening to put them away or abandon them).
⊙ *Physical* – beating or any physical act that was violent or intentionally injured you, severe sadistic forms of punishment.
⊙ *Sexual* – when any adult or older child coerces you into any sexual contact or involves you in their own sexual gratification.
⊙ *Neglect* – when a parent does not feed a child or look after their basic needs (clothing, shelter or attending to their medical needs). Being left alone before they are able to look after or protect themselves, or being exposed to potential danger. Children can also be emotionally neglected (not given affection).

E
X
E
R
C
I
S
E
9.1   **Parenting questionnaire**

Listed on the following page are statements that you might use to describe your parents. Read each statement and decide how well it describes them. Choose the highest rating that describes your mother, then your father, when you were a child and write the number in the spaces before each statement. If someone substituted as your mother or father, a step parent or foster parent, please rate the scale for that person (cross out mother or father and state the substitute). If you did not have a mother or father leave it blank, but even if you did not know one parent for long it may be helpful to try and answer these questions.

1 = completely untrue
2 = mostly untrue
3 = slightly more true than untrue
4 = moderately true
5 = mostly true
6 = describes him/her perfectly

Mother	Father	Description
_____	_____	1 Loved me. Treated me as someone special
_____	_____	2 Spent time with and paid attention to me
_____	_____	3 Gave me helpful guidance and direction
_____	_____	4 Listened to me, understood me, shared feelings with me
_____	_____	5 Was warm and physically affectionate [*ed]
_____	_____	6 Died or left the house permanently when I was a child
_____	_____	7 Was moody, unpredictable or an alcoholic
_____	_____	8 Preferred my brother(s) or sister(s) to me
_____	_____	9 Withdrew or left me alone for extended periods [*ab]
_____	_____	10 Lied to me, deceived me or betrayed me
_____	_____	11 Abused me physically, emotionally or sexually
_____	_____	12 Used me to satisfy his/her needs
_____	_____	13 Seemed to get pleasure from hurting people [*ma]
_____	_____	14 Worried excessively that I would get hurt
_____	_____	15 Worried excessively that I would get sick
_____	_____	16 Was a fearful or phobic person
_____	_____	17 Overprotected me [*vh]
_____	_____	18 Made me feel I couldn't rely on my decisions or judgement
_____	_____	19 Did too many things for me instead of letting me do things on my own
_____	_____	20 Treated me as if I was younger than I really was [*di]
_____	_____	21 Criticised me a lot
_____	_____	22 Made me feel unloved or rejected
_____	_____	23 Treated me as if there was something wrong with me
_____	_____	24 Made me feel ashamed of myself in important respects [*ds]
_____	_____	25 Never taught me the discipline necessary to succeed in school

Mother	Father	Description
_____	_____	26 Treated me as if I was stupid or untalented
_____	_____	27 Didn't really want me to succeed
_____	_____	28 Expected me to be a failure in life [*fa]
_____	_____	29 Treated me as if my opinions didn't count
_____	_____	30 Did what he/she wanted regardless of my needs
_____	_____	31 Controlled my life so that I had little freedom of choice
_____	_____	32 Everything had to be on his/her terms [*sb]
_____	_____	33 Sacrificed his/her own needs for the sake of the family
_____	_____	34 Was unable to handle many daily responsibilities
_____	_____	35 Was unhappy a lot and relied on me for support and understanding
_____	_____	36 Made me feel that I was strong and should take care of other people [*ss]
_____	_____	37 Had very high expectations for him/herself
_____	_____	38 Expected me to do my best at all times
_____	_____	39 Was a perfectionist in many areas; things had to be just so
_____	_____	40 Made me feel that almost nothing I did was quite good enough
_____	_____	41 Had strict rigid rules of right and wrong
_____	_____	42 Became impatient if things weren't done properly or quickly enough
_____	_____	43 Placed more importance on doing things well than on having fun or relaxing [*us]
_____	_____	44 Spoiled me, or was over-indulgent, in many respects
_____	_____	45 Made me feel I was special, better than most other people
_____	_____	46 Was demanding; expected to get things his/her way
_____	_____	47 Didn't teach me that I had responsibilities to other people [*et]
_____	_____	48 Provided very little discipline or structure for me
_____	_____	49 Set few rules or responsibilities for me
_____	_____	50 Allowed me to get very angry or lose control
_____	_____	51 Was an undisciplined person [*is]

Mother	Father	Description
_____	_____	52 We were so close that we understood each other almost perfectly
_____	_____	53 I felt that I didn't have enough individuality or sense of self separate from him/her
_____	_____	54 I felt that I didn't have my own sense of direction while I was growing up because he/she was such a strong person
_____	_____	55 I felt that we would hurt each other if either of us went away from the other [*em]
_____	_____	56 Worried a lot about the family's financial problems
_____	_____	57 Made me feel that if I made even a small mistake something bad might happen
_____	_____	58 Had a pessimistic outlook; often expected the worst outcome
_____	_____	59 Focused on the negative aspects of life or things going wrong [*nv]
_____	_____	60 Had to have everything under control
_____	_____	61 Was uncomfortable expressing affection or vulnerability
_____	_____	62 Was structured and organised; preferred the familiar over change
_____	_____	63 Rarely expressed anger
_____	_____	64 Was private, rarely discussed his/her feelings [*ei]
_____	_____	65 Would become angry or harshly critical when I did something wrong
_____	_____	66 Would punish me when I did something wrong
_____	_____	67 Would call me names (like stupid or idiot) when I made mistakes
_____	_____	68 Blamed people when things went wrong [*pu]

Young (1994) (abbreviated)

E
X
E
R
C
I
S
E
9.2 What does this tell you about your childhood?

If you were abused or neglected by any parental figure, how has this affected you?

E
X
E
R
C
I
S
E
9.3 The following questions relate to 14 of the 15 schema we looked at in Chapter 7.

1–5	emotional deprivation [ed],
6–9	abandonment/instability [ab],
10–13	mistrust/abuse [ma],
14–17	vulnerability to harm and illness [vh],
18–20	dependence/incompetence [di],
21–24	defectiveness/shame [ds],
25–28	failure to achieve [fa],
29–32	subjugation [sb],
33–36	self-sacrifice [ss],
37–43	unrelenting standards [us],
44–47	entitlement/self-centredness [et],
48–51	insufficient self-control or self-discipline [is],
52–55	enmeshment or undeveloped self [em],
56–59	negativity [nv],
60–64	emotional inhibition [ei],
65–68	punishment [pu].

Compare your scores to those you had for the schema questionnaire. If they differ much, you may need to review your answers to the schema questionnaire.

CONFRONTING WHAT HAPPENED

Just as a snake sheds its skin
we must shed our past over and over again

It may be necessary for people to confront their painful memories before they are able to move through depression, self-blame or self-hatred, or in order to manage their distress less self-destructively. Research evidence about the treatment of psychological problems shows that 'exposure' to distressing memories or emotions may be needed before we can tolerate them. When you are abused or traumatised, blocking out awareness of what's happening is a valuable survival strategy, but continuing to do this can lead to problems. You may end up using more and more extreme methods to block out memories and feelings, such as ritual cleaning, bingeing, vomiting, taking drugs, getting drunk or harming yourself.

This way of coping can become a problem when it happens in a way that you have no control over. This is known as dissociation. There are a range of dissociative experiences. These include episodes when you feel detached from yourself (depersonalisation) or when the world feels unreal (derealisation), blanking out (when you may have a memory lapse), seizures or blackouts. You may also have physical sensations which are fragmented memories of traumatic past experience.

Confronting painful memories may be necessary before you can

⊙ learn to tolerate them and the negative feelings linked to them, without self-destructive coping strategies;
⊙ re-evaluate your experiences – in particular who was responsible (i.e. those who abused you).

How this is done and who with is a sensitive matter. There are a number of self-help books available. *Toxic Parents* (Forward, 1989) is a good book to start with. Many people find that a therapist or counsellor, who can be neutral but supportive, helps give them the courage to go through this. They can provide the support needed to deal with the fear and distress which are often locked into the memories. It can also be important to have a witness who listens, is non-judgemental and gives them time and support. These were needed, but rarely available to the person at the time they were abused.

You may need to reduce your 'high-risk' behaviours to get yourself ready to do this work without escalating self-harm or substance misuse. Only go as far as you feel safe to and talk about ways of managing difficult feelings that this may bring up. Also you will not necessarily remember all the important things that have happened to you. If this is the case you will have to trust that you are dealing with it at the pace you can.

DEALING WITH CHILDHOOD ABUSE AND NEGLECT

If you have been sexually abused, there are many helpful books. *Outgrowing the Pain* (Gil, 1983) is short and particularly good for those who don't feel ready to work directly on their memories. *Breaking Free* (Ainscough and Toon, 1993) is a useful 'workbook' (not too long!) written by two experienced British psychologists and survivors they have worked with. This book will take you through the work suggested here in more detail. However, there are few self-help books written about other forms of abuse or neglect. We know from research (see Chapter 3) that neglect is equally important in the development of borderline problems.

On the basis of considerable research with survivors of child sexual abuse, Finkelhor (1986) summarises the effects of abuse in four areas. These effects can apply to all forms of abuse:

- ⊙ *Betrayal*. When an adult abuses or neglects a child they are betraying that child's ability to trust others. Most abusers have established a relationship with the child. If they were someone you were close to or loved, who should care for and protect you, especially your own parent, the betrayal is very profound and damaging. This may leave you either with a terrible loss and vulnerability to depression or anger which you may take out on yourself or others.
- ⊙ *Powerlessness*. Children who are abused by adults are relatively powerless, especially when it is a trusted adult. If the abuse is severe or repeated this will leave the child feeling ineffective or out of control, and these feelings are likely to carry over into adulthood. This can result in feelings of powerlessness over your emotions (depression or anxiety), over your body (which may lead to eating disorders), or in relationships and life in general (which can result in a cycle of further abusive relationships).
- ⊙ *Physical or sexual traumatisation*. Sexual or physical abuse can cause physical pain, leading to sexual or physical problems in adulthood.
- ⊙ *Stigmatisation*. Children who are neglected or abused often feel they somehow deserve to be abused, perhaps because they are told this, and that there is something different and bad about them. Those sexually abused get a sense that it is wrong because of the secrecy enforced by the abuser and as they grow up learn that sex between children and adults is shameful. Most survivors carry very bad feeling about themselves and feel different

from others. (If you ever harm yourself or abuse drugs or alcohol and have been sexually abused, you may have done so in an attempt to manage your feelings of shame or of being 'bad'.)

E
X **9.4**
E
R **Understanding the mind of a child**
C
I How old were you when you were abused?
S
E What were your expectations and knowledge of adults and of people who were supposed to care for you?

Discuss this in sessions. Thinking about this, what do you need to bear in mind now when trying to cope with difficult feelings associated with your abuse?

Finkelhor (1984) describes four steps before abuse occurs. Exploring each of these in sessions can be very helpful in re-evaluating the conclusions you came to about your abuse and who was responsible:

1 *The intention and motive to abuse.* This is stating the obvious, but it is important to locate the motivation for the abuse in the abuser.
   Why do adults abuse children? Think of all the possible factors which may be linked to an increased risk of abuse.

   Do you know any reasons contributing to why the person who abused you did?

2 *They have to overcome inhibitions not to abuse.* Most people find the abuse of children morally repugnant. Most abusers know that abuse is considered morally wrong and is illegal.
   How do people rationalise their abusive behaviour? (After thinking about this first, see the notes on page 132.)

   What about the person/people who abused you? How did they justify (or how do you think they justified) their actions?

3 *They create opportunities to abuse and hide what they do.* Most abuse happens behind closed doors and may involve getting the child alone. Abuse may be impulsive but can require careful planning in order that the abuser is not

discovered. Adults who sexually abuse children either know their victims or work at gaining their trust.

What do you know about the manoeuvres of child abusers in general?

How did the person/s who abused you get you on your own or keep what they did hidden from others?

4 *They have to overcome the child's resistance, by threat or domination.*

How do abusers get children to comply or submit?

What about your abuser/s? In what way did they dominate or overpower you?

If you were sexually abused, how did they get you to do what they wanted? What form of persuasion did your abuser/s use? Were you bribed or threatened in any way?

E X E R C I S E 9.5 Did you know that most children who have been abused do not tell adults, or only do so many years later. Why do you think this is?

Children who have been abused show their distress in some way. What signs were there that something was wrong for you? If you did try and tell, what happened?

E X E R C I S E 9.6 Write a list of all the reasons why you think your abuse happened.

Take each in turn and explore whether your conclusions are accurate in light of what you know about the people who abused you.

EXERCISE **9.7**

Now write all the reasons why the person/s who abused you was/were to blame.

Then write a list of all the reasons why you were not to blame.

EXERCISE **9.8**

For those who were sexually abused

One reason why children who've been sexually abused may feel guilty is if they have experienced pleasurable feelings. Some children respond sexually during abuse and can experience orgasms or pleasure. This can be very confusing and leave the person with a sense of guilt or shame. If this happened to you, it was because your body was responding as it is physiologically programmed to. It may have felt like a form of affection and feeling special to someone when they otherwise felt neglected. This can cause a lot of confusion and lead people to feel that there was something wrong with them, that they should not have enjoyed it.

Were any aspects of your experience positive or pleasurable?

How have you felt about this?

What do you need to remind yourself of about this?

COPING WITH FLASHBACKS AND NIGHTMARES

- Tell yourself you are having a flashback or nightmare, and that this is OK and very normal in people who have been traumatised.
- Remind yourself that the worst is over – it happened in the past and it is not happening now.
- It may help you to think of the abused part of you as a hurt child. This is not all of you. The adult part of you can comfort and reassure your 'hurt child'. Say soothing things to yourself.
- Try and orient yourself in the present. Focus attention on your environment, look in detail at what is around you. Make conscious contact with your own body or something else which is neutral or pleasant. Hold a stone in your hand. Stroke a cat. Stamp your feet. Listen to the sounds around you.
- Breathe calmly. Notice how you are breathing and take a few slow, calm breaths, holding the area above your navel and feeling it go up and down.
- If you have had a nightmare and woken up, stay still in bed and lie quietly – you may go back to sleep. If you don't, wait for a while before you get up. Breaking your sleep may increase your agitation and can easily become a habit. If you do get up do something gentle and soothing like making a warm drink and having a bath. Don't stimulate your mind. Try and go back to bed and lie calmly. Hopefully you will go off to sleep.
- If you are trying to avoid remembering something, it may need to be remembered, it may need to be faced or talked through before it can fade or be integrated. Flashbacks and nightmares can be a signal from your own mind to attend to something. Try writing down what comes to you in the flashbacks or nightmares and talking this through in sessions. Drawing or painting these images may also be a release.

CONFRONTING THE ABUSER AND FAMILY MEMBERS

Some people decide they want to break the wall of silence and tell their family, confront a parent who they feel failed to protect them or failed to intervene or to confront the abuser. Anger is an appropriate response. The expression of anger and speaking up to others is for most people a reversal of many years of silence and an avoidance or denial of the truth within the family. For some people speaking out is a way of finally refuting that they were in any way responsible and asserting their innocence – a powerful and symbolic act of throwing off shame or self-blame. It is better, however, not to do this impulsively and for you to talk through in sessions the possible outcome of you speaking out. It may not be helpful for you to tell any family members unless you know they will be supportive. You need to minimise the risk of once again feeling isolated and unsupported if you are not believed, blamed, if they trivialise what happened to you, ignore what you have said, or tell you it's over and it's time to get on with your life. These are all common responses by family members who may feel unable to deal with what you have raised. Perhaps they have ghosts of their own or cannot face the prospect of their failing to protect you, or they choose to remember a parent more positively because of the reasons we outlined above. We all need to believe in our parents.

Before confronting anyone you feel let you down or anyone who neglected or abused you, think about all the possible ways they are likely to react and how each of these would affect you. Think about the best way you can express what you want to say (e.g. by letter or to the person's face) and how this will affect the outcome. Ideally you need to have no expectations of what will happen. That way you won't be further hurt or disappointed. In order to reach that point you may need to do a lot of work on the issue. It may be better to make your statement by speech or in writing to someone who will listen and support you, such as a counsellor or support group.

EXERCISE 9.9

- Write a 'no holds barred' letter to anyone who neglected or abused you and anyone you feel failed to protect you. Don't censor what you feel. Write everything you feel. (This letter is not to be sent.)
- Read this letter to your therapist or key worker.
- Put the letter on your mantelpiece or somewhere private for a week or two. Imagine sending it. What thoughts, feelings and fears does this bring up? Discuss this in sessions.
- Make a decision whether you want to confront anyone. Discuss the possible outcome and how you would feel and cope. If you decide to go ahead, consider the pros and cons of speaking or writing to them.

If you want to speak to someone face to face, write down what you would like to say. If you want to write to them you will probably need to rewrite your letter.

OVERCOMING VICTIM PATTERNS IN RELATIONSHIPS – PARENTING YOUR HURT CHILD WITHIN

Penny Parkes (1990) describes how abuse survivors such as herself often sabotage good experience because of carrying a deep sense of guilt, fear and inadequacy:

As a young adult I wanted desperately to be loved and cared for. I wanted to feel special and important to someone . . . I couldn't see it then but I wanted a partner to come along and parent me as I should have been parented as a child . . . I would set emotional tests that a person would have to be a mind-reader to pass . . . saying to myself 'see that proves you don't love me'.

(Parkes, 1990)

She goes on to say how we can 'parent' ourselves. Whenever you feel vulnerable or upset, comfort the hurt child physically (e.g. by cuddling a teddy bear or pillow). Talk to the comfort object as though it were the hurt child within you.

EXERCISE 9.10 If you are troubled by painful memories you may find it helpful to construct a rescue scene in which the adult you rescues the child in a powerful unambiguous way. Discuss this in sessions. You will need to practise doing this for a minute or two twice a day for ten days. Imagine your rescue scene as if it is a video you are directing. When the image is very clear, bring to mind the painful memory then substitute the rescue scene. You can create a rescue scene for every different memory.

GROUPS

Groups for survivors of abuse can also be very helpful, but they usually focus only on sexual abuse. Such groups are available in most cities, either in mental health or voluntary services such as those provided by Rape Crisis, or independently. They can help you overcome the feelings of isolation that no one else can understand what you have been through and give you support over a longer period than an individual counsellor or therapist can. You also need to ensure that the people who help you are skilled and able to deal with what you need to share. Most importantly they should never have any sexual contact with you, and anyone who suggests this is acting inappropriately and unprofessionally. If this occurs I would recommend that you complain to the person's employing authorities or professional body.

NOTES

1 Other factors will also influence how affected you were (e.g. was the abuser your own parent)?
2 In 30–40 per cent of cases abusers have drunk alcohol.
3 Either they are a close relative or get to know the family (e.g. by baby-sitting), or gain access to children by working with them.
4 Children are taught that adults know best and tend to trust adults. Abusers rarely need to use force to coerce children.
5 Children do not tell because they do not think they will be believed or because they are frightened of what may happen. Some children are threatened (e.g. that a sister will be abused or that the family will break up). See Ainscough and Toon (1993, 46–47) for a list of why children don't tell and pp. 59–60 for a list of silent ways of telling. Those who do tell may not be believed. Children who have told and have not been supported feel further betrayed and may have more problems later in life as a result.

WARNING

The intention of this chapter is not for you to see yourself as a victim nor to blame your parents for your problems. This is an area where there is a lot of black-and-white thinking! Try and bear in mind:

⊙ Research shows that most people with borderline problems have been abused or neglected. However, not everyone with borderline problems has been abused or neglected. Some felt put down or controlled. Some people report that their parents have always been supportive of them, though these people are in a minority.

⊙ Your parents were most likely to have been doing their best in bringing you up and had problems of their own. Finding out more about their problems and upbringing may help you.

⊙ Ultimately, we have to accept what has happened to us. If you have been severely abused by your parents, who have never made amends or continue to mistreat you, it is probably best for you to have no contact with them. Otherwise it may be important for you to work at improving your relationship with them. They are the only parents you will have. (This applies equally to their memory if they are dead.) If you are concerned about this, discuss it in sessions.

MOVING ON

If you have been abused or neglected you may not feel able to leave the pain behind, but you can build your life up and look forward.

Pearls are made from a grain of sand which irritates the inside of a shell over and over and in the process builds into something of beauty. This may be a helpful metaphor for you. The shell can seem grey and plain but is protective, keeping you safe while you grow.

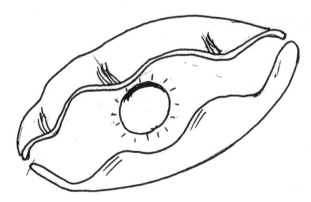

You are the pearl, perfect and beautiful within, growing through all the wear and tear of life.

REFERENCES

Finkelhor, D. (1984). *Child Sexual Abuse: New Theory and Research*. New York: Free Press.
Finkelhor, D. (1986). *A Source Book in Child Sexual Abuse*. Beverly Hills, Calif.: Sage.

Young, J.E. (1994). *Young Parenting Inventory*. New York: Cognitive Therapy Center of New York.

SUGGESTED READING

**Ainscough, C. and Toon, K. (1993). *Breaking Free: A Self-help Book for Adults who were Sexually Abused as Children*. London: Sheldon Press.

**Dolan, Y. (2000). *Beyond Revenge: Living Well is the Best Revenge*. London: Brief Therapy Press.

Dryden, W. (2000) *Overcoming Shame*. London: Sheldon Press.

**Forward, S. (1989). *Toxic Parents*. New York: Bantam.

**Gil, E. (1983). *Outgrowing the Pain*. Dover, UK: Smallwood. (This is an excellent introduction, especially for people who are not used to reading.)

Herbert, C. (1999). *Overcoming Traumatic Stress – A Self Help Guide Using Cognitive Behaviour Techniques*. London: Robinson & Constable.

**Kennerley, H. (2000). *Overcoming Childhood Trauma*. London: Robinson Publishing.

Parkes, P. (1990). *Rescuing the Inner Child. Therapy for Adults Sexually Abused as Children*. London: Souvenir Press.

Sanders, T.L. (1991). *Male Survivors*. Santa Cruz, Calif.: The Crossing Press.

(**highly recommended)

ORGANISATIONS

Breaking Free 020 8648 3500
Based in the Surrey area, Breaking Free provides a telephone helpline, face-to-face help, group work and support by letter and newsletter.

FAMAC (Female Adults Molested as Children) 01389 758 593
Based in Dumbarton. Contact Josie Riley.

Survivors, PO Box 2470, London SW9 9ZE
Helpline Mon. and Tues. (7–10 p.m.) 020 7833 3737
A national support organisation for male victims of sexual violence.

Survivors Network, 79 Buckingham Road, Brighton BN1 3RJ
Helpline 01273 720110

Basement Project, Lois Arnold, 82 Colston Street, Bristol BS1 5BB
0117 922 5801, or your local Rape Crisis Service

Review of Chapter 9

Please circle your answer to each of the following:

How much of the chapter did you read?

0%   25%   50%   75%   100%

Overall, was it

Very helpful

Helpful   Don't know   Not relevant to me   Unhelpful

Did you/your client complete Exercise 9.1?

Yes   No

Was it

Very helpful   Helpful   Don't know   Unhelpful

Did you/your client complete Exercise 9.2?

Yes   No

Was it

Very helpful   Helpful   Don't know   Unhelpful

Did you/your client complete Exercise 9.3?

Yes   No

Was it

Very helpful   Helpful   Don't know   Unhelpful

Did you/your client complete Exercise 9.4?

Yes   No

Was it

Very helpful   Helpful   Don't know   Unhelpful

Did you/your client complete Exercise 9.5?

Yes   No

Was it

Very helpful   Helpful   Don't know   Unhelpful

Did you/your client complete Exercise 9.6?

Yes   No

Was it

Very helpful   Helpful   Don't know   Unhelpful

Did you/your client complete Exercise 9.7?

Yes   No

Was it

Very helpful   Helpful   Don't know   Unhelpful

Did you/your client complete Exercise 9.8?

Yes   No

Was it

Very helpful   Helpful   Don't know   Unhelpful

Did you/your client complete Exercise 9.9?

Yes   No

Was it

Very helpful   Helpful   Don't know   Unhelpful

Did you/your client complete Exercise 9.10?

Yes   No

Was it

Very helpful   Helpful   Don't know   Unhelpful

Comments

Overcoming self-harm (the silent scream)

Self-harm is a common problem, though one which is difficult for people to admit as they may feel ashamed, stigmatised or 'crazy'. It may seem shocking to others, yet this is hypocritical as most of us do things, such as smoke cigarettes, which are harmful to us. Approximately 60 per cent of people with borderline problems self-harm. People harm themselves for a number of reasons. It is a way of managing intolerable distress. This may include feelings and beliefs about their own badness, in which case the self-harm can be a form of punishment. People often describe self-harm as giving a powerful physiological release of tension or stimulation. It may increase levels of endorphins which help reduce pain and induce a state of relaxation (Parkin and Eagles, 1993). It can also give a sense of control over feelings which are otherwise out of control, a way of externalising internal pain or chaos (Leibenluft, 1987), or getting anger out (Favazza and Conterio, 1989). It is rarely an attempt at suicide and can actually help to stave off attempted suicide (Babiker and Arnold, 1997).

Most people who self-harm have experienced abuse or neglect. Van der Kolk *et al.* (1991) studied 74 people with a range of mental health problems, including BPD. They found that chronic self-harm was most frequent among people with the most severe histories of separation and neglect and/or histories of sexual abuse. Experiences of separation and neglect were significantly associated with cutting. People with histories of prolonged separation and no memory of feeling cared about were least able to use inner resources to control self-destructive impulses. Similarly, Dubo *et al.* (1997) found that self-harm in people with BPD was associated with a history of sexual abuse or emotional neglect.

E
X
E
R
C
I
S
E | **10.1** | **Understanding self-harm**

How and when do you hurt yourself? Keep a diary and try and describe as clearly as you can the emotion you felt before you self-harmed (e.g. loneliness, sadness, shame) and how you felt after (e.g. calmer, better for punishing myself).

EXERCISE 10.2

The effects of self-harm

What are the consequences:

In yourself?

In your relationships with

⊙ family?

⊙ friends?

⊙ health care staff?

EXERCISE 10.3

The function of self-harm for you

Why do you think you self-harm? Is it because

⊙ it relieves tension;
⊙ it punishes you for feeling guilty;
⊙ it makes your pain seem real rather than just inside your head;
⊙ you want people to know how bad or angry you feel (which?), and you don't know how else to communicate this;
⊙ anything else?

ALTERNATIVES TO SELF-HARM

It is important to learn how to tolerate painful states and manage your distress without harming yourself. Discuss in sessions what you do at difficult times when you successfully avoid self-harming, and other possible things you could try as alternatives (see list at the end of the chapter). No one alternative will work all the time. You need a range of possible strategies. Make a list of these in the order you are most likely to use them. Keep this list on a card with you at all times. If needed, have more copies in a number of places (such as your handbag, bathroom). You don't need to say on the card what they are for. Whenever you are in a desperate state and feel like hurting yourself use your list. Make a promise to yourself to try three alternatives first, such as phone a friend, chew an ice cube, crush an egg in your hand, mark yourself with a pen instead. You may not be able to take the distress away but have to 'ride the wave' until it eases. If the impulse to self-harm is very strong, reduce the opportunity to act on it. Don't store tablets or keep razor blades. If you are doing this give them to your guide or someone you trust.

E X E R C I S E **10.4**   **The desire to stop**

Make a list of the reasons why you want to stop self-harming.

Keep this on a card and read it whenever you feel the urge to do it again.

EXERCISE 10.5 **Coping strategies**

Make a list of things you could do instead when you have the urge to self-harm. Brainstorm all the ideas you can. Nothing will work all the time so you need as many ideas as possible. (There are probably times you have had the urge to self-harm but have managed not to. What helped?)

When you have a list, go through it and write it in the order of which is most practical to do first.

Whenever you have the urge to self-harm, take out the list and remind yourself of your commitment to try and manage your problems differently. Every time you have the urge and don't do it you are building self-care and self-management skills. If the impulse comes over you quickly, use your list after you have self-harmed. You need to continue with this until the strategies have become internalised.

If you do hurt yourself here are some guidelines about how to deal with it.

SELF-CARE FOLLOWING SELF-HARM

Cutting

If the cutting is not deep you need to clean and dress the wound. You can get steri-strips from a chemist. If the wound is deep, particularly if the muscle is exposed, you should go to your nearest Accident and Emergency department. You also need to make sure you are up to date with tetanus injections.

Overdosing or ingestion of poisonous substances

You should always get checked by a doctor following an overdose or ingestion of obvious toxic substances, reporting what you have taken, how much and when. You may be in a very serious condition if you have severe nausea and vomiting. They may need to take a blood test and may decide to empty your stomach. Ideally you should give them any more medication you have. You should not be prescribed anything which is toxic such as tricyclic anti-depressants. If you are taking anti-depressants check which one. If it is toxic and you overdose regularly you should get this changed. If necessary you can get this from a different doctor (e.g. a psychiatrist or GP can change your medication). Under the Patient's Charter you also have a right to see a second consultant.

Burns

Minor burns should be immersed in cold water for at least 10 minutes. More serious burns should be seen by a doctor.

If you have anything which you can use to cause yourself further harm you should give these in to Health Service staff or someone you can trust to help you.

Attending A & E

People's experience in A & E is variable. If staff are abrupt or seem unkind it is usually because

⊙ they are frustrated that you have done this to yourself when they have other patients to treat who they feel are not responsible for their injuries;
⊙ they believe, usually wrongly, that if they are kind to people they are more likely to do it again.

If you are not given the physical care you believe you need you should consider making a complaint. Understanding the reasons if people are brusque with you will, I hope, help you not to take this personally. It may help you to think that you are only going there for your body to be treated.

SELF-SOOTHING

In order to be able to better manage painful states you need to understand and learn how to take care of your 'hurt inner child'. Showing interest and giving time to a child is how we show them love. When your mood changes take a few minutes to ask your 'inner child' how they are. Maybe they will say 'I'm lonely' . . . 'I'm frightened' . . . 'I'm tired' . . . 'I'm feeling rejected'. Ask them what they want or need. Can you comfort yourself in any way? For example, cuddle up with a hot water bottle, a teddy bear or your cat. Crying or rocking are natural responses to deep distress and may help. But you need to bring yourself out of it after a while, otherwise you can get stuck in a state of deep distress and despair. You may need to comfort yourself in words, saying things like 'it'll be OK', 'it's different now', 'you'll get by', 'this feeling will change', 'it's not always this bad'. Doing this regularly will help you learn what your true needs are and how to take care of yourself. Although you probably long for someone to take care of you at these times there may be no one there who can do that. Depending on people in that way can be problematic. Being 'parented' can rarely fulfil an unmet need from the past, so even if someone tries to take care of you this usually becomes problematic. You can get dependent on them. They can get bewildered or fed up. So it is very important that you learn to nurture yourself. This is a skill which comes with practice.

PRACTISE THESE WAYS OF TRYING TO RELEASE BAD FEELINGS

- ⊙ Screaming into a pillow or over very loud music.
- ⊙ Going to the beach and screaming at the waves or throwing stones into the sea.
- ⊙ Breaking china against a wall (keep a pile of cheap old china from jumble or car boot sales in the cupboard for this purpose).
- ⊙ Think of one word which best expresses how you feel. Write it down over and over.

POSSIBLE ALTERNATIVES TO SELF-HARM

Try the following:

- Write down why you want to hurt yourself, and why you don't want to and why you don't deserve to.
- Do something loving to yourself instead. Massage the place you want to hurt.
- Speak to someone. Call a help line – your local one in the mental health service, Samaritans or a self-harm help line (see p. 144).

If you feel you have to hurt yourself, do one or more of these first:

- Cut something else instead of yourself (e.g. a towel).
- Crush an egg on your hand.
- Hold an ice cube in your hand.
- Bite on something very hard (e.g. a piece of leather).
- Mark or write on yourself with red ink. (Get a washable marker pen.)

REFERENCES

Babiker, G. and Arnold, L. (1997). *The Language of Self-injury*. BPS Books.

Dubo, E.D., Zanarini, M.C., Lewis, R.E. and Williams, A.A. (1997). Childhood antecedents of self-destructiveness in borderline personality disorder. *Canadian Journal of Psychiatry*, 42(1), 63–69.

Favazza, A.R. and Conterio, K. (1989). Female habitual self-mutilators. *Acta Psychiatrica Scandinavica*, 79, 283–289.

Leibenluft, E. (1987). The inner experience of the borderline self-mutilator. *Journal of Personality Disorders*, 1(4), 317–324.

Parkin, R.J. and Eagles, J.M. (1993). Blood letting in bulimia nervosa. *British Journal of Psychiatry*, 162, 246–248.

van der Kolk, B.A., Perry, J.C. and Herman, J.L. (1991). Childhood origins of self-destructive behavior. *American Journal of Psychiatry*, 148, 1665–1671.

BOOKS FOR PEOPLE WHO SELF-HARM

*Arnold, L. and Magill, A. (1998) *The Self-Harm Help Book*. Abergavenny, Wales: The Basement Project.

Harrison, D. (1995) *Vicious Circles: An Exploration of Women and Self-harm in Society*. GPMH Publications, 380–4 Harrow Road, London W9.

The Hurt Yourself Less Workbook. Available from National Self-Harm Network, PO Box 16190, London NW1 3WW.

Pembroke, L. (ed.) (1994). *Self-harm. Perspectives from Personal Experience: Survivors Speak Out.*
*Strong, M. (2000). *Bright Red Scream*. London: Virago.
* recommended

GROUPS

There are many self-help groups and helplines across the country for people who self-harm. Contact Bristol Crisis Service for Women (BCSW, PO Box 654, Bristol BS99 1XH), The National Self-Harm Network (PO Box 16190, London NW1 3WW) or your local MIND association.

HELPLINE

BCSW Friday and Saturday evening (9 p.m.–12.30 a.m.) 0117 9251119.

NEWSLETTER

Shout (c/o PO Box 654, Bristol BS99 1XH).

Review of Chapter 10

Please circle your answer to each of the following:

How much of the chapter did you read?

0%   25%   50%   75%   100%

Overall, was it

Very helpful   Helpful   Don't know   Not relevant to me   Unhelpful

Did you/your client complete Exercise 10.1?

Yes   No

Was it

Very helpful   Helpful   Don't know   Unhelpful

Did you/your client complete Exercise 10.2?

Yes   No

Was it

Very helpful   Helpful   Don't know   Unhelpful

Did you/your client complete Exercise 10.3?

Yes   No

Was it

Very helpful   Helpful   Don't know   Unhelpful

Did you/your client complete Exercise 10.4?

Yes   No

Was it

Very helpful   Helpful   Don't know   Unhelpful

Did you/your client complete Exercise 10.5?

Yes   No

Was it

Very helpful   Helpful   Don't know   Unhelpful

Comments

Me and me

Learning to take care of, be with and like yourself

Our self-image and beliefs about ourselves are learned when we are children. When we were young we absorbed and believed all the messages that we were given. These were direct (e.g. 'you bad child') and indirect (e.g. being ignored if you are hungry or upset may lead you to think that you are unlovable).

SELF-NEGLECT

People with histories of neglect may grow up feeling they are not important and haven't learned how to take good care of themselves. Self-neglect can take many forms.

Do you neglect yourself in any way?

- ◉ your diet and health;
- ◉ failing to protect yourself (e.g. when you have sex, who you hang out with, getting into cars with strangers);
- ◉ your environment;
- ◉ your appearance;
- ◉ living for the moment and not investing in your future or long-term welfare (e.g. getting into debt, risking pregnancy, breaking the law).

Can you identify when these patterns began and how you learnt them?

Do you feel able to take better care of yourself in any way? Talk this over and see what steps you could take.

LEARNING TO BE WITH YOURSELF

Most people don't think about the fact that they have a relationship with themselves, but in fact this relationship will shape our health and happiness more than any other. Many people have difficulty being alone without feeling bored, restless or lonely. This problem is not unique to you, but tackling it is central to overcoming borderline problems. Being comfortable in your own company is one of the most important goals for change.

Being with yourself is not just the absence of others. It is about being present with yourself (i.e. conscious) and aware of your needs and treating yourself how everyone likes to be treated – thoughtfully, with care and respect. This is not sentimental. It is the foundation of everything else you would like to achieve. Being with yourself in a mindful way can restore your energy, enable you to slow down and reflect on things and give you the space to be creative. Relationships with others are unlikely to work unless we can also be with ourselves this way.

EXERCISE **11.2** What feelings come up for you when you are alone?

How do you deal with them?

How could you cultivate pleasure in your own company? Brainstorm all the possibilities.

Ask other people if they enjoy their own company and how.

SOME PRACTICAL TIPS ABOUT LEARNING TO BE WITH YOURSELF

⊙ Plan how to use your time when you are alone.
⊙ Try to do a variety of things by yourself – at home (reading, preparing a meal) and out (going for a walk, having a cup of coffee in town).
⊙ Do something occasionally to challenge the belief that you can only do it with someone else (e.g. go to the cinema or out for lunch). This will help you feel more independent.
⊙ Plan some human contact too but not out of desperation. Choose who you would like to visit or phone. Consider doing this later after being with yourself for a while. (Remember that they may not be in.)
⊙ Consider other ways of giving yourself something, such as cooking yourself a nice meal (act against the 'what's the point if it's just me' attitude). Also, consider other ways of feeling connected to people such as listening to the radio, watching the TV or writing to someone.
⊙ If you get really panicky and lonely, remind yourself who does care about you. Have a drawer or somewhere where you keep things which will help you feel cared about (cards etc.). Photos may be helpful, but only if you can feel the person with you in spirit or memory. Try keeping a comfort box of mementoes, statements, cards, etc. that help you feel good.
⊙ If it is really difficult then build it up gradually. For example, if being alone over a weekend feels impossible, plan to spend an hour alone every weekend and then increase this gradually.

SELF-ESTEEM

Many people have a poor sense of self-worth, which can be a major factor in mental health problems. Poor self-esteem will predispose you to develop mental health problems (anxiety, depression, eating disorders), and affect your relationships. Experiences which knock your self-esteem can trigger these problems, and if you have low self-esteem you will find it harder to get over these problems. (People who are depressed tend to have a negative outlook of themselves, others, or the world and the future.)

EXERCISE **11.3** If you did a life line in Chapter 3, take it out again and plot on a graph your self-esteem at different stages in your life. Were there any times in your life you felt better about yourself? When did you feel worst? Can you link these to any events or experiences?

11.4 The 20 statements test

1 Make a list of 20 words you would use to describe yourself. Put a ring around the six you think best describe you.

2 Put the list in categories (e.g. physical appearance, character, intelligence).
Talk through your self-image in each of these areas. What evidence do you have for this? Is this a balanced view? (Most people are good and bad, average in looks or intelligence.) How do you think others see you?

3 Now take each of these areas and write three positive things about yourself that you like or feel good about. If you find this difficult discuss it with someone you trust.

4 Write here the six words which you think describe you. (We did an exercise like this in Chapter 7.)

These are your 'core beliefs' about yourself. What is your view of yourself like? Is it likely to give you low or high self-esteem? If it is negative, what do you need to do to move on and feel better about yourself? Are there any goals you feel able to make (e.g. to stop blaming yourself, to learn to accept your body size, to stop trying to change your physical image). These will help you feel better about yourself.

CHANGING HOW YOU FEEL AND THINK ABOUT YOURSELF

Liking ourselves is something we can build or cultivate. Here are some exercises to begin this process. Like any change, if you want to feel better about yourself you have to work at it.

EXERCISE 11.5 What do you feel are your achievements in life? What are you proud of?

Write these down and share them. Don't give in to those thoughts and feelings that say nothing (remember that thinking pattern – dismissing the positives!). You know how hard your achievements were for you.

EXERCISE 11.6 What qualities or strengths do you have? If you can't think of any, think what others might say of you?

EXERCISE 11.7 What are your hopes and aims for the future? (Self-esteem grows when we set ourselves challenges and meet them.)

FALSE SELF-ESTEEM

All of us learn ways to try and boost our self-esteem. Many of us hide our true feelings about ourselves because we want to be popular and liked. Society (our culture) teaches boys and girls different ways of trying to boost their self-image. Boys are usually taught to be strong, tough and gain self-esteem through sport and practical skills. Girls tend to learn to feel good about themselves in two ways – through helping or pleasing people and being attractive. Whilst enjoying make-up and fashion can be harmless fun, it can also cause great suffering for those who feel unattractive. Some women (and a few men) go to extreme lengths to try and change their appearance – plastic surgery, starving themselves. Others get into debt buying clothes they may not even wear.

EXERCISE **11.8** How have you tried to boost your self-esteem?

Does it work? How long do the feelings last? What is the cost (to your health, your pocket, your peace of mind)?

There are many books about self-esteem now available. (This reflects how widespread low self-esteem is.) Some of the most useful are written by Lynda Field (1993, 1995). She describes how self-belief shapes our lives.

Another negative triad is helplessness, hopelessness and low self-esteem. If you feel that life is difficult, which it probably has been for you, it is easy to feel helpless and hopeless. If you also have low self-esteem, this is a recipe for going nowhere!

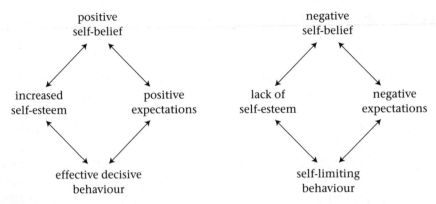

E
X
E
R
C
I
S
E

11.9 What are the negative thoughts which contribute to and maintain your low self-esteem?

Can you write affirmations (positive statements about yourself) which would help to change these. This may be very difficult for you and you will probably need help with this. Affirmations need to be personally meaningful and believable, not idealistic or sentimental. Put your affirmations on a card and practise them two or three times a day (e.g. when you go to bed and when you wake up). Try to say them out loud if you are alone, otherwise you can say them silently to yourself.

E
X
E
R
C
I
S
E

11.10 State all the things in your life you are proud of. You need to accept and forgive yourself for the mistakes you have made in life – we all make them! Remember that what we do (or did) is not who we are. This is a universal truth shared by all the world religions.

Finally, remember one of the truths about emotions – that they change. So a certain amount of fluctuation in your confidence and how good you feel about yourself is quite natural.

When people carry very negative beliefs about themselves, these feelings can be triggered in certain situations. They may be so intense and difficult-to-manage that people binge-eat or take drugs or alcohol to numb the feelings, or punish themselves by purging (vomiting or taking laxatives) or harming themselves. Increasing your sense of self-worth or self-esteem will help you tolerate bad states without blaming or wanting to punish yourself.

Improving your self-esteem does not happen overnight, but you can make a commitment to stop blaming yourself or putting yourself down. There is no quick solution. Things you may need to do include:

- learning to stand up for yourself and be assertive;
- breaking cycles of victim thinking and behaviour;
- changing thought habits and beliefs about yourself that are negative or self-blaming;
- stop putting yourself down;
- re-evaluating anything which you blame yourself for.

Which of these do you need to tackle? Work through these in sessions.

DEVELOPING YOUR OWN IDENTITY

One of the criteria for BPD is a poor sense of self. This is defined as

an identity disturbance characterised by markedly and persistently unstable self-image or sense of self. There are sudden and dramatic shifts in self-image, characterised by shifting goals, values and vocational aspirations. There may be sudden changes in opinions and plans about career, sexual identity, values and type of friends . . . Although they usually have a self-image that is based on being bad or evil, individuals with this disorder may at times have feelings that they do not exist at all. Such experiences usually occur in situations in which the individual feels a lack of a meaningful relationship, nurturing and support.

(DSM-IV, 1994)

Do you think any of this applies to you? If so, discuss how you can develop a more stable sense of who you are.

Here are some ideas:

- Don't throw yourself hook, line and sinker into things. For example, if you meet someone and think you are made for each other don't move in with them immediately. Relationships which escalate that quickly tend to crash quickly too.
- Be cautious when you have strong feelings for someone. This is not necessarily love. Love is something which grows with time and commitment. Attraction is based on many things, some of which may not be healthy.
- You may feel very strongly that a decision or change is right or someone new is your life partner. Ask yourself if you have felt that way before or about anything or anyone else? Looking back over your life, are those feelings reliable? Did your feelings change?
- Keep your options open. Don't burn your bridges. For example, if you move in with someone you could lose your own place, then if the relationship doesn't work out find yourself homeless.
- If you are attracted to someone of the same sex, don't assume you are gay. You may be bisexual or gay, but you are likely to be confused about your sexual orientation. Talk this over with people you can trust.
- If you make new friends or you have an affair or romantic relationship, don't give up all your other friends and activities. Try and keep a range of friends, interests and activities. Don't put all your eggs in one basket. Try not to spend all your leisure time with one person. If that relationship doesn't work out you will be left vulnerable.
- If you have the urge to change course in life (e.g. start a college course or leave one, have a baby), take your time. Talk it over with a number of different people.
- Recognise that you are unlikely to get a healthy sense of identity by trying to achieve it through how you look (the clothes you wear, your hair, etc.). We all do this to some extent, but external features are no substitute for an internal sense of values and personal identity.

Underline those you think will be useful to you.

BOOKS ON SELF-ESTEEM

Branden, N. (1992). *The Power of Self-Esteem*. Deerfield Beach, Florida: Health Communications Inc.

Burns, D. (1985). *Intimate Connections: The New Clinically Tested Programme for Overcoming Loneliness*. New York: William Morrow.

Fennel, M. (1999). *Overcoming Low Self-Esteem*. Oxford: Oxford Stress and Trauma Centre.

Field, L. (1993). *Creating Self-Esteem*. Shaftesbury, Dorset: Element.

Field L. (1995). *The Self-Esteem Workbook DSM-IV*. Shaftesbury, Dorset: Element.

Hartman, C. (1987). *Be-good-to-yourself Therapy*. New York: Warner Books.

McKay, M. and Fanning, P. (1992). *Self-Esteem: A Proven Program of Cognitive Techniques for*

Assessing, Improving and Maintaining Your Self-esteem (2nd edition). Oakland, Calif.: New Harbinger Pubs Inc.

Warner, M.J. (1999). *The Complete Idiot's Guide to Enhancing Self-Esteem*. New York: Alpha Books.

AUDIOTAPES

Building Self-Esteem (Nathaniel Branden, SSEA4000).
Superconfidence Workout (Gael Lindenfield, SHA 9000).
Feeling Good (Bill Wiles: two-tape set, self-esteem and assertiveness, SSHA4400).

REFERENCES

American Psychiatric Association (1994). *Diagnostic & Statistical Management IV*. Washington, DC: American Psychiatric Association.

Review of Chapter 11

Please circle your answer to each of the following:

How much of the chapter did you read?

0%   25%   50%   75%   100%

Overall, was it

Very helpful   Helpful   Not relevant to me   Don't know   Unhelpful

Did you/your client complete Exercise 11.1?

Yes   No

Was it

Very helpful   Helpful   Don't know   Unhelpful

Did you/your client complete Exercise 11.2?

Yes   No

Was it

Very helpful   Helpful   Don't know   Unhelpful

Did you/your client complete Exercise 11.3?

Yes   No

Was it

Very helpful   Helpful   Don't know   Unhelpful

Did you/your client complete Exercise 11.4?

Yes   No

Was it

Very helpful   Helpful   Don't know   Unhelpful

Did you/your client complete Exercise 11.5?

Yes   No

Was it

Very helpful   Helpful   Don't know   Unhelpful

Did you/your client complete Exercise 11.6?

Yes   No

Was it

Very helpful   Helpful   Don't know   Unhelpful

Did you/your client complete Exercise 11.7?

Yes   No

Was it

Very helpful   Helpful   Don't know   Unhelpful

Did you/your client complete Exercise 11.8?

Yes   No

Was it

Very helpful   Helpful   Don't know   Unhelpful

Did you/your client complete Exercise 11.9?

Yes   No

Was it

Very helpful   Helpful   Don't know   Unhelpful

Did you/your client complete Exercise 11.10?

Yes   No

Was it

Very helpful   Helpful   Don't know   Unhelpful

Comments

Me and other people

People with borderline problems often have problems in relationships, particularly in close relationships. You are likely to long to feel cared for and may cling to people at times, or do things in order to try and secure a sense of feeling cared for. You may also find close relationships threatening in some way – you may feel dominated or controlled in a relationship or find that your anxiety or tendency to get angry goes up. You may find yourself repeating patterns from early relationships, desperately seeking care or rejecting people, or oscillating between these two extremes. Understanding and addressing these problems is very important; building and keeping successful relationships will help you to feel OK. Research shows that many people with BPD report that they have got better with the help of a close relationship (Links and Heslegrave, 2000).

HISTORY REPEATS ITSELF

Certain feelings will come up again and again in close relationships. You are likely to deal with these feelings in certain ways. How you do this will have a significant impact on your relationships with people. For example, you may often end up feeling let down by people. There are a number of ways you could deal with this. You may withdraw (cut the person dead and never speak to them again). You may get angry or vengeful (do something, or fantasise about doing something to hurt them and 'pay them back' for hurting you). You may feel this is confirmation that you are unlovable, blame yourself and punish yourself in some way.

12.1 What patterns can you observe in your relationships – in your feelings and in your behaviour? Go back to your schema grid (p. 96). How do each of your schema affect your relationships?

How would you describe the way the most important people in your childhood treated you or the way you experienced them (positive and negative)? Write down the key words that sum this up for you (e.g. controlling, ignored me, absent, abusive, loving).

How did you respond to that? For example, if people tried to control you, were you rebellious or compliant (trying to do what they want), and inwardly angry and resentful?

Has this pattern recurred in any other relationship? If so, who with?

Here are some common relationship problems you may have:

HEROES AND VILLAINS

Many people with BPD are searching for a perfect caregiver who will be all-giving, 100 per cent kind and reliable. The need to experience such care can be so great that when someone gets close, or tries to care, you may see them as everything you ever wanted – your hero or knight in shining armour.

Inevitably however, such expectations will not be met. When you are disappointed the crash may be so intense that you then experience the person as totally unreliable, untrustworthy – in short, a villain. Putting people in either all good or all bad categories is known as 'splitting'.

SEARCHING FOR CARE: THE MERRY-GO-ROUND

Remember the black-and-white thinking we covered in Chapter 7. This pattern of thinking is very relevant if you have problems in this area. Overcoming these problems will involve modifying that thinking and learning to recognise that people can care *and* disappoint you.

The habit of seeing people as either good or bad, a hero or villain, probably comes from your early experience. If an experience was too painful you may have blocked it out of your mind or memory so you can still feel good. Then when you feel hurt all the painful feelings flood back and it feels all bad. This is natural in young children, but if this way of coping continues into adulthood it causes problems. Most relationships are good and bad. When we feel let down by someone we need to hang on to the times they have been reliable. When we feel hurt we need to remember the times they have been good to us. There will be times when we need to evaluate whether a relationship is good for us. It may be right to end a relationship. You are more likely to evaluate this accurately when you can weigh up all experience equally. It's not a good idea to make such a decision impulsively when you feel intense negative feelings towards them.

E X E R C I S E **12.2** Do your feelings towards people change? What are the key emotions you experience in relationships, positive and negative?

How do you behave or treat people when you feel they have let you down?

MISTRUST

You may feel very hurt or let down by important people in your life. If you were abused you will probably find it very difficult to trust people, especially if you were abused by your parents and the abuse was severe or happened for many years. You may also have had later relationships which were based on shared addictions, lust or loneliness which left you open to be treated badly again. This will have reinforced your mistrust of people.

You may imagine and fantasise how someone may hurt or let you down and this can lead to various problems – anxiety or 'paranoid thinking' are common. Some people deal with their anxiety about someone deceiving or rejecting them by trying to control the other person – wanting to know their every move, interrogating them. (This is particularly likely if you are a man.) You may be so mistrustful and jealous that you sabotage the relationships you have and eventually drive the other person away. This may be a 'schema' for you, and an example of black-and-white thinking (see Chapter 7).

If you avoid relationships this is one way of not getting hurt. It also prevents you from revising your 'schema' by having better relationships and can leave you isolated and lonely. It is important to re-evaluate this schema and recognise that not everyone is necessarily going to treat you badly.

EXERCISE **12.3** Write a list of anyone who has ever:

- been kind to you
- shown you affection
- helped you

Before you go to sleep at night recite to yourself at least one good experience you have had that day. If you can't think of one for that day remember one from the past.

POSSESSIVE JEALOUSY

You may remember from Chapter 3 that many people with borderline problems have experienced loss or rejection. This may leave you feeling very anxious about being left again or having repetitive intrusive thoughts about your partner deceiving you. One way some people try and cope with the fear of being abandoned again is to try and control their partner. These problems can place great strain on a relationship and if unchecked can contribute to its downfall. Often people take the easy way out of a relationship and form another relationship first. This would leave you having your worst fears confirmed – that you cannot trust your partner not to go off with someone else ('all women . . .' or 'all men . . .'). The first step is to become of aware of the problem.

E X E R C I S E **12.4** **Jealousy checklist**

Are you a jealous person? If so how do you deal with it? How do you try and control your partner? Do you do any of the following?

⊙ imagine they look at people they are sexually attracted to. (Do they or do you exaggerate this in your mind?)
⊙ avoid going out with them or avoid doing other things because of such feelings
⊙ insist on doing things with them so you can keep a watchful eye on them
⊙ interrogate them when they come home
⊙ check their pockets/handbag
⊙ listen in on their phone calls
⊙ exhort promises out of them
⊙ ask them to tell you in detail what they have or haven't been doing
⊙ try and stop them doing things where they may flirt or be flirted with
⊙ make wild accusations
⊙ verbally or physically attack them
⊙ follow or stalk them
⊙ lock them in rooms or your home, or tie them up

Are you ready to own the problem as yours? If your partner has been unfaithful, what is the most appropriate way for you to deal with that (forgive them, consider leaving the relationship, get more support so you are less dependent on them)? If no, what are you willing to do to tackle the problem? You will need to reduce and eventually give up the above behaviours and find other ways of dealing with your fears. Read the chapter on anger for some ideas about how you could manage these feelings better.

REJECTING OTHERS

You may at times avoid or reject people because when you get involved you

⊙ become anxious;
⊙ feel bored;
⊙ feel controlled by the other person;
⊙ fear rejection or abandonment.

Most people with borderline problems don't stay like this for long because they are desperate to feel cared for and find it difficult to be alone. You may reject someone then desperately want them again. If you lose interest or find someone else you may drop someone. If you feel you are going to be rejected you may precipitate the end of the relationship (e.g. by going off with or sleeping with someone else) so you can feel more in control.

EXERCISE **12.5** Have you ever rejected someone? Why did you do this?

Have you ever pushed someone away because you were hurt, then tried to get them back again?

POOR BOUNDARIES

Do you know what boundaries are? Boundaries are what help give you a sense of identity independently of others. They are very important if we are to survive emotionally in relationships. Otherwise we can get engulfed and lose the sense of who we are.

E
X **12.6** Think of an example of a close relationship you know where
E there are healthy boundaries. Describe that relationship.
R
C
I Now think of a relationship you know where there are poor
S boundaries. (This may be one of your own.) What is that like?
E

What are your boundaries like in relationships?
Do you tend to

⊙ tell people a lot about yourself when you hardly know them?
⊙ spend all your spare time with someone and very little time
  alone?
⊙ contact the person frequently?
⊙ have sex with people when you haven't known them very long?

Do you ever phone at unsocial hours?

What were your parents' boundaries like?

⊙ with each other;
⊙ with other people;
⊙ with you.

How do you think you could improve your boundaries in
relationships?

Think about setting limits with

⊙ time (not spending too long with the same person),
⊙ place (cultivate and regularly spend time in your own space),
⊙ physical contact (how can you keep some of yourself in reserve
  rather than give all of yourself physically).

What would help you do this?

PROJECTING NEGATIVE FEELINGS ONTO OTHERS

If your parents' boundaries were poor they may have acted out their feelings and moods on you (e.g. blamed you for things when they were fed up about something else). If injustices like this were done to you it will have had a number of effects. One is that you are likely to do the same. Do you tend to have someone you hate or blame and direct your anger and hostility towards them? Do you pick rows with people when they don't necessarily deserve it? When you are feeling negative and angry try not to project this onto others or take it out on yourself. (Middle way again!)

GETTING INVOLVED WITH PEOPLE WHO TREAT YOU BADLY OR LET YOU DOWN

Some people get into relationships which repeat experiences of neglect or abuse. There may be many reasons for this. You may be desperate to feel cared about and get involved with anyone who 'picks you up'. You may be easily taken in or a poor judge of character. You may feel so bad about yourself that you feel you don't deserve someone who would treat you well. You may crave excitement and find the people who would treat you better boring and those who are likely to treat you badly exciting. You may be drawn to someone who is like one of your parents (e.g. a substance abuser or someone abusive to you) in the hope of putting right what was wrong in your childhood. (This is very unlikely to happen. Instead you will be a victim or a martyr!) Does this ring any bells? If so you need to evaluate your current relationships and whether they are likely to meet your needs or repeat this pattern. What role, if any, might you play in that pattern? You may be needy and therefore stay with someone rather than being alone (a 'victim' role), or you may contribute to violent rows with your own anger and provocation.

Having better relationships will involve

⊙ choosing people who are less likely to treat you badly;
⊙ changing your life style so you are more likely to meet such people, and avoiding people who are likely to treat you badly;
⊙ recognising that as an adult your behaviour contributed to bad things that happened in the relationships;
⊙ handling your problems better so you are less likely to sabotage good relationships or for them to end in a way that leaves you feeling hurt, rejected or abandoned.

CLINGING TO OTHERS FOR COMFORT AND CARE

Everyone who has experienced significant loss or neglect in childhood has painful states in which they long to be looked after or parented again. Do you experience a state of overwhelming distress when you are desperate to be looked after or cared for? Can you recognise this state and describe it? You are likely to feel at these times that someone must make you feel better or help you; that you cannot feel better unless that happens. However, looking for someone else to rescue you will become a problem. If you have unmet needs in your past you are likely to experience that state again and then search for care. If you don't get the care you want and feel you need, your way of communicating your distress may escalate (e.g. by threatening suicide or acting on suicidal urges). This may get you care sometimes, but if it happens repeatedly people are unlikely to take you seriously and may become fed up or angry with you. You could end up like the boy who cried wolf so many times that when there really was a wolf no one believed him.

EXERCISE 12.7 Can you track how different states in your relationships may happen in a sequence, one conditioned by another? See if you can plot this in a circle. This will help you become more aware of what is happening when you feel hurt or angry or things go wrong in your relationships.

TRYING TO PLEASE OTHER PEOPLE

Your behaviour in relationships will vary depending on how close you get to someone. This is true for all of us. You are likely to get very distressed and angry at times with people in close relationships (families and partners). In less close relationships (friends) you will probably try not to do this and may try hard to please them in order to keep their friendship.

How do I try to please people?

Are my relationships equal?

What is the effect of this for me/for them/for my relationship?

YOUR RELATIONSHIPS WITH PROFESSIONAL STAFF

Many of the relationship issues that come up for people with borderline problems arise in their relationships with staff. When you first meet someone you may pour out everything to them in the hope that they will help you. This may be overwhelming. Alternatively, you may begin feeling guarded or wary and not tell them very much at all. Then if they stick with you (and pass the trust test!), old hopes and longings may surface that you will be cared for and that someone will understand you. You may form an intense attachment which generates strong feelings towards the person. You may hope that person is going to save you or believe you cannot cope without them. This may have a number of consequences. You may be devastated if they miss an appointment or go on holiday. At some point your contact with them will draw to an end and you may not be able to cope with the thought of never seeing them again. People deal with such feelings in a number of ways. Maybe you will avoid feeling abandoned (again) by ending the relationship yourself. 'Dropping out' is very common, but not helpful for you. Alternatively, you may try and prolong the relationship by not getting better, or telling them about more and more problems. If you have idealised someone, it is inevitable you will feel disappointed in them or let down by them at some point. Then you may withdraw completely and never want to see them again, or you may feel angry and get enraged with them. You may feel unable to tell them how you feel, aware that your feelings may be too intense. You may be afraid that if you tell them your true feelings they will feel overwhelmed and abandon you.

Of course staff aren't perfect. They may not cope well with such intense emotions and may well not give you the support you need, or they may get angry with you. Either party may act out their disappointment or anger directly or indirectly. Talking about negative feelings in any relationship is difficult and – by British people anyway – often avoided. Some of your suspicions may be quite accurate (for example, when you feel the other person can't cope with you and discharges you or passes you on to someone else). These are very complex issues. If someone doesn't feel they can help you successfully, it may be best for them to pass you to someone else. But naturally this may feel like another broken relationship or rejection.

EXERCISE **12.9** This exercise focuses on your part in relationships. This does not mean that difficulties were necessarily your fault or that the staff were perfect.

On the left, list all the people you have seen regularly about your problems. This may include your GP, a counsellor, psychiatrist, nurse, therapist or psychologist. On the right, write down what feelings you have/had towards them. You may have different contradictory feelings.

Did you find it difficult to trust them and therefore not tell them things?

Did you have strong positive feelings towards them? If so how did you deal with that?

Did you have strong negative feelings towards them? If so how did you deal with that?

Did you tell them how you felt, and what was their response?

Did you ever feel angry towards them? How did your anger come out?

Did you ever try to influence what happened to you by doing or saying certain things (e.g. making overt or covert threats)?

Did you ever lie to them or exaggerate anything?

How did the relationship end?

Were the reasons for this explained to you? Did you take it personally?

What are your thoughts about what happened now you know your patterns better?

You may have some of these feelings in your relationships with staff now. You will have shared a lot of intimate feelings and details about yourself so it is natural for you to feel close. It is helpful to talk about any fears or anxieties you have, and this will be especially important as the sessions draw to an end.

EXERCISE 12.10 Talk in sessions about any feelings you have towards those involved in your treatment; any anxieties or concerns. How can you best deal with them?

MANAGING DISTRESS WITH THE MINIMUM BURDEN ON RELATIONSHIPS

When you are hurt *you* need to parent your 'inner child'. This does not come easily because alongside the hurt is a deep longing for the care you never had, or never had reliably. This is like a 'frozen need' in that no amount of care by others will take away the hurt. In order to manage these states better, we have to learn to love and care for ourselves. You need to do this physically – comfort and cuddle yourself, maybe give yourself a warm bath. You also need to do this verbally, saying, for example 'It's going to be OK . . . Don't worry, you'll feel better in a while . . . I'll never leave you . . . I'm here for you. I'll take care of you.'

If you find this difficult you may need to practise this when you are not upset. Visualise yourself as an infant or child. Imagine yourself when you were hurt or lost, then visualise yourself as an adult taking care of you, soothing, comforting and protecting you.

Being able to soothe ourselves is also vital to the survival of intimate relationships. Most of us in our early relationships are unconsciously or otherwise looking for the parenting we missed out on. Intimate relationships rarely survive such impossible expectations. Adult relationships do not work if a lot of the time we are trying to get the parenting we wanted or needed in the past. Frozen needs tend to be insatiable. Whilst genuine caring relationships help to make us feel more loved and secure, we may never fully replace what we didn't receive as children. Trying to make others fill this 'hole' is ultimately unproductive – they may withdraw, thereby reinforcing our feelings of abandonment. Or they may have their own reasons for trying to rescue us; but this can lead to other problems. If we do not respond how they hope we will, e.g. if we get angry with them for not getting it right, then this can cause mutual disappointment or conflict.

EXERCISE **12.11** How could you take care of yourself when you are acutely distressed?

Create a visual picture of doing that. Practise using that image twice a day for a couple of minutes. If you can establish that image successfully in your mind you will be able to use it to comfort yourself when you are mildly distressed and eventually when you are severely distressed.

Many people cry when they are very upset, and this is absolutely fine. Young children sob and wail and you may need to do this too. However, you also need to keep some of your awareness away from your distress otherwise you can regress into a state of distress which is rehearsing rather releasing. You need to learn the difference. One way you can tell is how able you are to trust someone. If you are pushing someone away, saying 'you don't care, you don't understand', it's likely that your attention is shut down and you are locked into the 'hurt child' role. If you can grieve and comfort yourself, or allow someone to comfort you, then you're learning to keep your attention balanced. Another way is to notice whether your actions are skilful or not, as you have been doing in the diary. Getting angry with others or hurting yourself is repeating what was done to you. This is very important. Old hurts have a powerful pull, trying to convince you that that is how it really is (e.g. that nobody loves you). Think of this as an old recording of an early experience which can be triggered later in life when we feel hurt or let down. When you are in an emotionally charged state it is important to remember that your perception of reality can distort. It is shaped by what we called schemas (see Chapter 7). *Wise mind* will help you to calm down and feel better sooner, and limit the possible damage you can do to yourself or your relationships. Accepting the pain and not re-enacting these old roles will be fantastic progress. It will ease with practice, but this will take time.

Another important principle is to try not to *act on* your distress. This is addressed in more detail in the final three chapters. Acting on feelings of neglect and abandonment could lead to suicidal behaviour such as overdosing or threatening to harm yourself in an attempt to elicit care (see Chapter 10). It is common for people to act on anger by behaving in ways that are destructive to themselves, to others or to property (see Chapter 13). All of these responses have been learnt but are counter-productive. They are not likely to have the result you want. For example, the first time you take an overdose people may be worried and concerned about you (though not always). But if you do this a number of times, people may get 'compassion fatigue'. As a result they may take your needs *less* seriously or feel angry towards you rather than caring.

You need to be careful about how much you expect from people when you are distressed (i.e. not seek re-parenting). But, we all need people who we trust and admire and are role models for us. It is also important for you to build some relationships with people who you can turn to for help.

SOME TIPS FOR GETTING ON WELL WITH PEOPLE

⊚ Try to always treat others with respect. When you feel hurt this is a cue to manage your feelings.
⊚ If there are problems in a relationship, don't brood about how the other person should be different or keep telling them how you think they should be. Work on changing yourself not the other person. They are unlikely to respond to moans and groans! Taking responsibility for managing your side of things will be a good model for them. Change in one person can make a shift in a pattern of interacting and enable things to get better.
⊚ Think of ways you can foster harmony and co-operation, and set yourself goals towards this.
⊚ You will need to develop trust. Relationships cannot function without it. If someone really isn't trustworthy don't invest too much in that relationship.

REFERENCES

Links, P. and Heslegrave, R. (2000). Prospective studies of outcome. Understanding mechanisms of change in patients with borderline personality disorder. *Psychiatric Clinics of North America*, 23(1), 137–150.

SUGGESTED READING

Bruno, F. (1997). *Conquer Loneliness*. New York: Macmillan.
Burns, D. (1985). *Intimate Connections. The New Clinically Tested Program for Overcoming Loneliness*. New York: Morrow and Co.

de Angelis, B. (1992). *Are You the One for Me? Knowing Who's Right and Avoiding Who's Wrong*. London: Thorsons.

Dickson, A. (1982). *A Woman In Your Own Right*. London: Quartet Books.

Goldhor-Lerner, H. (1989). *The Dance of Intimacy*. New York: Harper & Row.

**Norwood, R. (1986). *Women Who Love Too Much*. London: Arrow.

(** Highly recommended)

Review of Chapter 12

Please circle your answer to each of the following:

How much of the chapter did you read?

0%   25%   50%   75%   100%

Overall, was it

Very helpful   Helpful   Don't know   Not relevant to me   Unhelpful

Did you/your client complete Exercise 12.1?

Yes   No

Was it

Very helpful   Helpful   Don't know   Unhelpful

Did you/your client complete Exercise 12.2?

Yes   No

Was it

Very helpful   Helpful   Don't know   Unhelpful

Did you/your client complete Exercise 12.3?

Yes   No

Was it

Very helpful   Helpful   Don't know   Unhelpful

Did you/your client complete Exercise 12.4?

Yes   No

Was it

Very helpful   Helpful   Don't know   Unhelpful

Did you/your client complete Exercise 12.5?

Yes   No

Was it

Very helpful   Helpful   Don't know   Unhelpful

Did you/your client complete Exercise 12.6?

Yes   No

Was it

Very helpful   Helpful   Don't know   Unhelpful

Did you/your client complete Exercise 12.7?

Yes   No

Was it

Very helpful   Helpful   Don't know   Unhelpful

Did you/your client complete Exercise 12.8?

Yes   No

Was it

Very helpful   Helpful   Don't know   Unhelpful

Did you/your client complete Exercise 12.9?

Yes   No

Was it

Very helpful   Helpful   Don't know   Unhelpful

Did you/your client complete Exercise 12.10?

Yes   No

Was it

Very helpful   Helpful   Don't know   Unhelpful

Did you/your client complete Exercise 12.11?

Yes   No

Was it

Very helpful   Helpful   Don't know   Unhelpful

Comments

13

Managing and reducing anger

People with borderline problems often experience intense anger and either feel they musn't express it (because it is wrong or dangerous) or are unable to contain it safely and tend to take it out on others verbally or physically. You may have a problem with anger for a number of reasons. You may carry a lot of anger inside you because of things that have happened in your life and how others have treated you. You may have been the victim of other people's anger or grown up witnessing others act out their anger uncontrollably. Many people with borderline problems or impulsive behaviour have been physically abused or witnessed violent anger as children. Either you learnt anger was wrong, so you suppress it and tend to take it out on yourself, or you didn't learn how to process angry feelings safely, so it builds up then explodes and tends to hurt others.

Learning how to manage your anger is very important. It can destroy close relationships or add to feelings of self-hatred or shame. We tend to assume that anger is a negative emotion which people do not enjoy. However, this is not always the case. Anger strengthens the ego and this can feel very positive. It may help you get your own way or feel strong instead of feeling vulnerable. In men in particular it can be 'instrumental' – getting what you want by bullying (but at a price). Like other states in people with borderline problems it can be very 'addictive'.

13.1

Anger inventory

Look at the emotions diary, which hopefully you have been keeping regularly!

Generally, when do you get angry?

Do you get angry with particular people? If so who?

Why do you think that is?

What do you do when you get angry?

How has anger affected your life?

⊙ your state of mind

⊙ your relationships

Have you ever got in trouble with the law? If you have, I highly recommend the book *We Are All Doing Time* (Lozoff, 1985).

Have you ever physically hurt someone?

Have you ever threatened to hurt someone?

How have you hurt people emotionally or verbally?

Continue to keep the emotions diary, focusing on when you feel angry and recording any time you get angry with yourself or others. Start to become more aware of the signs of when you are *becoming* angry.

There are four steps involved in dealing with anger:

1 Recognising it.
2 Owning it – acknowledging it is your feelings and problem.
3 Containing it without taking it out on others or yourself.
4 Allowing it to fade or releasing it appropriately.

Learning to do 1 and 2 are necessary before you can achieve 3 and 4.

RECOGNISING WHEN WE ARE ANGRY

You may think you know when you are angry, but if you behave destructively at times it is likely that you do not recognise when your anger first starts. There are different types of anger which we may call hot or cold. Hot anger tends to erupt and lead to conflict or violent behaviour. Cold anger is more long-lasting (e.g. when you stonewall someone and cut off all contact with them). Hot anger is the most destructive, so is best *not* acted on. (This does not necessarily mean suppressing it.)

E
X
E
R **13.2** What are the signals that you are feeling angry?
C
I
S
E

⊙ physical feelings, facial expressions, mannerisms

⊙ emotional feelings

⊙ behaviour towards others

Write down as many as you can.

Ask people who know you how they can tell when you are angry (see end of chapter for list after you have thought about this yourself).

OWNING OUR ANGER

Anger is a feeling, a response. How people respond varies. When you are angry the anger is yours. The other person may have done something that pushed your button or treated you in a way that justified your anger (e.g. if someone neglected or abused you as a child). But you have to accept responsibility for your feelings and especially for *how you deal with those feelings*. This may be very difficult for you to accept, but is essential if you are to make progress. You may think other people are the cause of your anger. When you are angry you may blame yourself (which may trigger self-harm or other self-destructive behaviours). Alternatively, you may blame others. This may trigger a hot row or a cold war between you and the other person (you cutting off the person to avoid dealing with your angry feelings or the potential conflict). This is an example of 'black-and-white thinking'. Remember 'the middle way'. This is what you need to work at achieving when managing angry feelings. This will help you to handle situations assertively rather than aggressively (see pp. 190–91).

Remember that the other person may see it differently

One way to help us own our anger is to think about the other person's perspective. When you feel mistreated, you probably think that you are right and they are wrong, and if anyone challenges your view on it they are saying you are wrong and the other person is right. Remember the styles of thinking in Chapter 7. Which style of thinking is this?

If you want to overcome intense anger, seeing situations from the other person's point of view is essential.

SETTING LIMITS TO WHAT WE DO WITH OUR ANGER

Intense negative emotions can become destructive *if they are acted on carelessly*. The intention here is not to make you feel guilty or bad but to realise that when you act on or act out your anger it is you (too) that gets hurt. Anger may be exciting, but unless you can set limits on the extent to which you act on it, it will wreak havoc with your relationships and ruin your peace of mind! Are you ready to make a commitment to not hurt others or yourself? We all fail to keep commitments at times but the intention is important and one you will need to repeat to yourself many times.

E
X **13.3** Write down how you act on your angry feelings (hot and cold).
E
R
C
I
S
E

        Think about your speech and actions to others and your inner speech and actions towards yourself.

        How would you like to be different?
Are you ready to make a commitment to how you are going to try and change?

        Discuss what steps you will need to take to achieve this.

You may feel the only choice you have is to give vent to your anger or suppress it. What would be the 'middle way'? – perhaps stating that you are angry. This may be less satisfying than punching someone, but it is more satisfying than saying nothing and keeping your anger simmering inside you.

Damage limitation!

Action

Are you ready to make a commitment to give up physically hurting others or yourself? Breaking property is better than hurting people – if your anger is really intense this may be the only alternative. But it can also escalate your anger as well as discharge it. The ultimate aim is to prevent yourself getting so enraged that you need to vent it in such ways.

Speech

Speech has a very powerful impact in our relationships. Whilst I wouldn't recommend you suppress your anger, it may be unwise and unskilful to vent it verbally. Leave the situation, or use the mindfulness techniques we discussed in Chapter 6 before addressing someone you are very angry with (see pp. 68–71). When you are calmer and can be assertive then talk, but don't just let yourself vent your spleen. Are you ready to make a commitment to give up verbally abusing others?

Time out

This is a very important strategy for preventing yourself from behaving in a destructive way when your anger escalates. If you are ever violent to others you will need to go somewhere safe where you can calm down, reduce your level of physical arousal (see Chapter 6), then use the techniques described below. If you are 'losing it', you need to leave the situation and take 'time out'. This will involve recognising when you are about to 'lose it'. To develop this skill you need to keep a diary every time you are angry and become aware of your anger as it develops (i.e. before it escalates). Once it has reached a certain pitch it will be very difficult for you to control it, so you need to choose what to do before your anger is this intense. You can only do that if you are aware of when you are angry earlier in the cycle.

If you get violent with your partner then you will need to discuss time out with them, where you go, how long for, what happens when you come back. When you have agreed a time, *stick to it*. This means you have to give up being vengeful. It will also help you to use the time out rather than just seethe. (When you go back you have to handle the situation better.)

If you have attempted suicide in the past you may need to agree a rule that you don't go off but do something else instead. Time out won't help you or your partner calm down if you go off and harm yourself.

13.4   **Your anger escalator**

Getting angry can be like being on an escalator – your anger goes up and up. If you rated your anger using a scale of 1–10, what would be the signs for you (in feelings and behaviour) at each step? Try this yourself then see the example at the end of the chapter.

1

2

3

4

5

6

7

8

9

10

Continue with your diary, using this rating scale. Review your scale once you have been using it.

At what point on your escalator will you be so angry that you need to take time out, but still aware enough that you can realise this and choose to do it? Practise recognising exactly when you reach this pitch. Make a commitment that as soon as you reach this point you will take time out. Discuss the situations where you are likely to get this angry (e.g. the pub, your home, your boyfriend's/girlfriend's home). Where can you go to take time out? It needs to be far away enough for you to calm down without going back and fighting again. You will need to take responsibility for this yourself – that is, you leave; you do not make the person you are angry with leave.

Self-talk or inner speech

Once you have learnt to refrain from acting out your anger in how you behave and speak you can then become aware of the 'tape' playing in your head. Remember the role of thoughts and beliefs in our emotions which was introduced in Chapter 7?

E X E R C I S E **13.5** Continue noticing and recording in a diary when you angry. Now focus on the thoughts you have. Try and record your inner speech. This will be thoughts such as 'I hate you, you, b . . .' or 'I hate myself – I'm bad', 'How dare you!', 'Nobody treats me like that!' Discuss these in sessions and use the techniques outlined in Chapter 7 to tackle the thought patterns.

Imagery and fantasies

Another way emotions are triggered is by images. What images are in your mind when you are angry? Do you have images of hurting people or yourself? If so you will need to change these. Do you have fantasies of what you would like to do or say to someone to get revenge?

E X E R C I S E **13.6** Continue with the diary but focus now on the images in your mind. Discuss the likely effect of these images and how you could change them.

Managing your anger

Here are some ideas. Not all of these will work for you, but some will if you do them regularly and for long enough. You need to try them then construct your own personal plan for dealing with your anger. You will need to discharge the tension, calm down and relax and change your perspective or the way you are thinking.

What can help:

⊙ Physical release (intense exercise, a brisk or long walk).
⊙ Switching your attention; for example, listening to relaxing music (sing to it or recite the words of a song), watching TV, going somewhere else. To distract yourself from a powerful emotion like anger you need to involve yourself as much as possible.
⊙ Have a shower or a bath. Use aromatherapy oils.
⊙ Breathing exercises.
⊙ Count from 1 to 10.

Changing what you think or say to yourself

⊙ Don't repeat over and over how you are wronged and how you hate the other person.
⊙ Think about how you will feel in an hour's time, a day's time, etc.
⊙ Remember your commitment to yourself to manage your problems differently.
⊙ Ask yourself what this anger is doing to you.
⊙ Remind yourself what your ultimate goals are for yourself or that relationship. What is it you really want?
⊙ Ask yourself 'How am I distorting things – am I black-and-white thinking, taking things personally, exaggerating?' (Keep a list of the thought habits you identified in Chapter 7.)
⊙ Let go of trying to get your own way or convincing the other person you are right.
⊙ Let go of wanting revenge for being or feeling hurt yourself.
⊙ Accept that arguments are usually caused by both parties.
⊙ Think about the other person's perspective. How are they feeling right now?
⊙ Write a few positive self-statements which will help you (see suggestions at end of chapter).

EXERCISE **13.7** Which of these have ever worked for you? Try them out.

Make your own personal list and write it on a card.

Make a commitment to use these strategies. If they don't work take time out until you are calmer.

RELEASING ANGER

There is no single right way of expressing anger. Different ways of expressing anger have different effects. What happens to your anger? Do you try and hold it in? If so, where does it go? If it comes out, how? Do you hurt yourself? Do you hurt others?

An important principle in how we release anger is

> *to not harm others or yourself; to minimise the harm to others or yourself*

Next, does what you do release anger or rehearse/reinforce it (i.e. does it tend to deflate your anger or fuel it)? A second principle then is

> *to release your anger, not rehearse or reinforce it*

13.8 Brainstorm all the ways anger can be let out.

Put them in the following four categories:

	Harmful to others	Safe to others
Releases anger		
Rehearses/ reinforces anger		

Safe ways of releasing anger

- ◉ Screaming or yelling (you can drown out the sound with loud music).
- ◉ Throwing stones into the sea.
- ◉ Shouting at the sea.
- ◉ Intense physical exercise.
- ◉ Punching cushions.
- ◉ 'Strangling' a towel.

Any other ideas?

EXERCISE 13.9

Personal action plan

Put together your own personalised plan for managing and reducing anger

The times I'm likely to get angry are when:

I know when I'm angry because of the following signs:

When I'm angry I have the following thoughts, or say the following to myself:

When I'm angry I behave in the following ways:

The reasons I would like to change are:

I will try to:

    think or say the following:

    behave in the following ways:

I will try to calm myself by

I will try to release my anger safely by

What else is important to you?

ADVANCED ANGER MANAGEMENT SKILLS

When you feel you can manage your anger without hurting yourself or others here are some further skills you can develop. The first is to apply these skills in relationships.

EXERCISE **13.10** **Assertiveness versus aggression**

What is the difference between assertiveness and aggression?

Write down three examples of each.

Look at each example in more detail. What would be an assertive response or an aggressive response on each occasion?

Think of a time when you have been assertive? How did you deal with the situation?

How did that make you feel?

What was the outcome?

Now think of a time when you were aggressive?

How did that feel (at the time and later)?

What was the outcome?

What are the important differences between assertiveness and aggression?

Learning to have less violent rows

EXERCISE 13.11 How do you behave when you have a row or argument? Be honest with yourself. Write down all the things you might do? What is the effect of this?

⊙ on the other person at the time

⊙ on your own state of mind

⊙ on your relationship

Are you willing to take responsibility for changing your part in this?

If so how could you fight 'more cleanly'?

Think of what you could do differently at each stage through which a row escalates.

The following will help you row 'hurt-free':

⊙ Speak one at a time. Try and listen to the other person and think about their point of view. Don't give someone the silent treatment or talk non-stop. You need to talk a bit and listen too.
⊙ Pause before you speak or act; stop, think and plan.
⊙ Own your feelings (I feel angry . . . I feel as if . . .) Change accusations into requests. Use more 'I' statements and fewer 'you' statements. For example, instead of saying 'you don't care about me', you can say 'I feel very hurt because I feel I'm not important to you.' For example, don't say 'You are never there when I need you', but 'I really need you. Please try and support me. It would mean a lot to me.'
⊙ Stand up for yourself, but in a friendly way. People with borderline problems are at times passive (e.g. when they are afraid of being disliked or rejected), and when they are angry tend to be aggressive. Try to find a middle way (see Chapter 7). For example, making statements like 'I'm sorry but I'd prefer not to do that. I don't want to offend you but I need to state my point of view.'
⊙ Avoid generalisations 'you always . . . you never . . .'

⊙ Say what you would have liked them to have done rather than attack or criticise them.
⊙ If you tend to get aggressive, keep your distance.
⊙ Try to maintain respect for the other person. This means when you attack or criticise you apologise. Try to say I'm sorry, I love you, I apologise, I'm confused (i.e. risk being vulnerable and showing that you care).
⊙ Walk away when you feel angry to try and cool off.

Which of these could you do? Put a star by them and try to do them next time you have a row.
   Try not to:

⊙ Shout. This does not help communication and is likely to make the other person upset or angry. If you shout don't swear.
⊙ Claim you know what the other person feels or thinks. Ask them and listen. Ask for clarification first (e.g. 'are you saying . . .?'). You may assume someone is insulting or rejecting you or has a particular motive, which may not be true.
⊙ Bawl them out, blame or attack.
⊙ Drag up old grievances.
⊙ Go for the jugular, using something you know will hurt them.
⊙ Make threats of any kind (to end the relationship, hurt yourself, kill yourself).
⊙ Hit them.

Which of these do you do? Put a cross next to them. Which are you willing to give up?

Working through the layers

You probably have layers of anger that have built up over many years: people who were angry with you, things that happened to you that shouldn't have, things you saw which made you angry. Added to these layers will be your own anger habits. Every time you have rehearsed anger in thought, speech or action you will have reinforced it. Our thoughts fuel anger – the belief that you are right, that you have been wronged, the outrage and sense of injustice; the righteous indignation. Your anger towards others who you feel don't treat you well also comes from expectations that someone can meet all your needs or put things right for you. You will need to work at your anger one layer at a time. You cannot do this all at once or change overnight. This is a lifetime's task, but even small progress will bring its rewards. You will suffer less and your relationships will improve.

EXERCISE 13.12 Remember a time when you felt warm feelings toward the person you are angry with or a time when they were kind to you. If you cannot remember such a time, remember someone else who you feel caring towards, get a sense of that feeling then visualise the person you are angry with and generate that feeling towards them. Think about when you felt loved by your partner or loving towards them.

Practise doing this twice a day for a week when you are not angry. Then see if you can use it when you feel angry towards someone.

Cultivating alternative states of mind

If you carry a lot of intense anger it is unrealistic to expect yourself to reduce it when it is severe and has you in its grip. You may at times have to sit it out, keeping to your commitment to yourself of what you will not do (hurt others or yourself). Another way to work at this is to cultivate alternative emotions. To wean ourselves off being angry we need to develop other qualities which are less intense. In time we will experience their benefit and value. There are positive states of mind which are natural to human beings but get interfered with and lost. They are all natural antidotes to anger. It is very difficult to feel these simultaneously with anger. (Try it!)

- ⦿ *Loving kindness*. Love makes the world go round! Love is something we can develop through thinking about others, doing things for them, the community or the planet.
- ⦿ *Compassion*. This is the feeling of empathy for those who are suffering. This could be for others or ourselves. This is the quality we can experience when someone we care about is hurt, or we hear about people in famine or war.

⊙ *Joy*. This is a sense of pleasure which 'brightens us up'; pleasure in simple ways (e.g. the sound of a bird singing, the colour, fragrance and beauty in a flower).

⊙ *Calm, peace*. This is probably the quality which is most strange to you. Have you ever felt it? Where, who with? Many people take marijuana or other drugs in search of this, but that can lead to other problems and isn't something we can rely on because it is not within ourselves. (What if your supply ran out or you couldn't afford it?)

E X E R C I S E **13.13** Think about what small things you could do to develop these 'mind states'. (This is for your benefit!). For example, smile when you meet your neighbours, look at a photo of someone you love, walk around a park and look at the flowers. List as many possibilities as you can.

Put a star by those you would like to do more.

APPENDIX

Signals of being angry

⊙ Tensing up – your jaw or knuckles or stomach.
⊙ Stress symptoms – headaches, stomach pains.
⊙ Impaired concentration – can't focus on other things, ruminating about someone or something they did or said (which has angered you).
⊙ Physical agitation ('hopping mad'), shaking, pacing up and down.
⊙ Avoiding eye contact, going quiet, sulking.
⊙ Drinking more alcohol, smoking, etc.
⊙ Raising your voice.
⊙ Swearing or name calling.

Example rating scale

1 mild irritation	6 throw something
2 feel pissed off	7 damage something
3 grumpy, grouchy	8 hit someone
4 pick a fight	9 hurt someone badly
5 scream and shout	10 beat someone up

Positive self-statements

Stay cool
The feelings will pass
In a week's time I won't even remember this
Here I go again, feeling wronged/victimised, etc.
Maybe I'm not in the right
Listen to yourself!
It's me that suffers
It's only pride that's stopping me from feeling better
Beneath the anger I feel really hurt
It's OK to cry

REFERENCES AND FURTHER READING

Davies, W. (2000). *Overcoming Anger and Irritability*. London: Constable & Robinson.
Dryden, W. (1996). *Overcoming Anger*. London: Sheldon Press.
Golhor-Lerner, H. (1992). *The Dance of Anger*. London: Pandora Press.
Lindenfield, G. (1993). *Managing Anger*. London: Thorsons.
Lozoff, B. (1985). *We Are All Doing Time*. Durham, NC: Hanuman Foundation.
McKay, M., Rogers, P.D. and McKay, J. (1989). *When Anger Hurts*. Oakland, Calif.: New Harbinger.
Thich Nhat Hanh (1991). *Peace is Every Step. The Path of Mindfulness in Everyday Life*. London: Bantam Books.

WEBSITE ON MANAGING ANGER

http://www.apa.org/pubinfo/anger.html

Review of Chapter 13

Please circle your answer to each of the following:

How much of the chapter did you read?

0%   25%   50%   75%   100%

Overall, was it

Very helpful   Helpful   Not relevant to me   Don't know   Unhelpful

Did you/your client complete Exercise 13.1?

Yes   No

Was it

Very helpful   Helpful   Don't know   Unhelpful

Did you/your client complete Exercise 13.2?

Yes   No

Was it

Very helpful   Helpful   Don't know   Unhelpful

Did you/your client complete Exercise 13.3?

Yes   No

Was it

Very helpful   Helpful   Don't know   Unhelpful

Did you/your client complete Exercise 13.4?

Yes   No

Was it

Very helpful   Helpful   Don't know   Unhelpful

Did you/your client complete Exercise 13.5?

Yes   No

Was it

Very helpful   Helpful   Don't know   Unhelpful

Did you/your client complete Exercise 13.6?

Yes   No

Was it

Very helpful   Helpful   Don't know   Unhelpful

Did you/your client complete Exercise 13.7?

Yes   No

Was it

Very helpful   Helpful   Don't know   Unhelpful

Did you/your client complete Exercise 13.8?

Yes   No

Was it

Very helpful   Helpful   Don't know   Unhelpful

Did you/your client complete Exercise 13.9?

Yes   No

Was it

Very helpful   Helpful   Don't know   Unhelpful

Did you/your client complete Exercise 13.10?

Yes   No

Was it

Very helpful   Helpful   Don't know   Unhelpful

Did you/your client complete Exercise 13.11?

Yes   No

Was it

Very helpful   Helpful   Don't know   Unhelpful

Did you/your client complete Exercise 13.12?

Yes   No

Was it

Very helpful   Helpful   Don't know   Unhelpful

Did you/your client complete Exercise 13.13?

Yes   No

Was it

Very helpful   Helpful   Don't know   Unhelpful

Comments

CHAPTER 14

Other problems

Casual sex, eating problems and hallucinations

You are likely to have a tendency to act on your urges, impulses, desires. We all do this of course – overeat, say things we regret. But getting on with people requires the ability to practise restraint, to hold back the urge to do or say things which are likely to antagonise or shock people. For example, if you shout at people every time you are angry with them, you won't get on well with them. If you have sex every time you feel attracted to someone, you are not likely to keep a sexual partner (most people want to be monogamous). Living within the law requires self-restraint, and some people with borderline problems get in trouble with the law because of the difficulty they have with impulsivity and anger in particular. (Many men with borderline problems end up in the penal system not the mental health services.)

Self-restraint may be a problem for you for a number of reasons. You may have a biological tendency to be more impulsive than other people. What is more likely is that you grew up in an environment where you did not experience healthy restraint. You may have witnessed or experienced sights which are not appropriate for children because your parental figures did not restrain themselves around you. They may have behaved aggressively, temperamentally, or indulged themselves in sex, drink or drugs. Alternatively, your only experience of restraint may have been harshly or punitively imposed so that you then became averse to any form of restraint and developed a 'I'll do what the hell I like' schema (see Chapter 7), or a 'If I must I won't/If I must not I will' script.

EXERCISE 14.1 In what ways are you impulsive? How was your learning self-restraint impaired? (How did your parental figures behave around you and towards you?)

You may need to explore this issue and discuss your attitudes and beliefs about it.

What areas of your behaviour would you benefit from in exercising more restraint? Some possible areas where you behave impulsively – eating, drinking alcohol, taking drugs, spending money, driving recklessly, getting angry and damaging property, having casual sex, hurting yourself, hurting others.

These behaviours may be *impulsive* (i.e. you get the urge and act on it without much reflection as to the possible consequences). They can also become *compulsive* in the sense that they can become a habit, that you plan them, and despite reflection on the consequences find it very hard to give them up.

You may not be aware of the risks and consequences of your impulsive behaviours. Perhaps you feel defensive, knowing that not everyone approves. Maybe you got criticised or bawled out for it when you were a teenager. Maybe you need to not feel any more bad about yourself than you do already, so you brush aside your concerns and tell yourself 'What the hell! Life is for living! You only live once! I may die young, but I'll die happy.'

SEX AND LOVE ADDICTION

Many people with borderline problems find themselves getting emotionally involved and/or having sex with people they hardly know. Whilst it is not uncommon for young people to experiment with intimacy and sex, if this pattern continues repetitively over a period of years it is an area you need to think about. There are a number of reasons why you may be over-willing to have sex with people. It may be that you get involved with people who want sex from you and don't know how to say no. You may also want sex yourself because it's a way of experiencing a sense of merging with another person, like when we are cuddled as babies.

EXERCISE **14.2** Write down all the aspects of sex that you enjoy on the left and all the aspects that concern you on the right.

Do you wish people would hold or cuddle you?

Does having sex meet that need?

Could you get cuddled more without having sex?

Think about the people you have got involved or had sex with.

How have they treated you?

How have the relationships ended?

How do you usually end up feeling about yourself?

EXERCISE **14.3** There are risks associated with casual sex. Can you list what they are. Write down as many as possible. Then put them in the order in which they concern you.

Check with the list at the end of the chapter.

EXERCISE **14.4** Make a list on the left of all the people you can remember having had sex with then write down on the right how you think you felt after each.

Now write down all the people you have felt affection from in your life. How do the two lists compare?

How many of the people you have had sex with have you also felt affection from?

What does this tell you?

When you have sex, are you searching for something? If so what?

How likely are you to meet your needs?

Is there any other way you could try to get these needs met?

EATING PROBLEMS

Many people with borderline problems have a problem with their body image at times, with binge eating and/or purging behaviours such as self-induced vomiting or laxative misuse. There are many reasons why you may develop an eating problem. Like most Western women, you may strive to lose weight in order to feel better about yourself.

If you are not in control of other areas of your life (like your emotions and behaviour) or feel bad about yourself, you may try to compensate by trying to be thin or under-eating so you feel successful or in control. You have had many problems which were overwhelming and often out of your control. It's natural that you want to focus on one thing in the hope that it's the solution to all your unhappiness – being slim. The media and culture we live in tells us that slimness leads to total happiness. Research shows that women with borderline problems who develop eating problems are likely to be those who have been abused as children. Extreme dieting, bingeing and purging are also strategies used to try and cope with intrusive memories and negative feelings, often towards oneself (see Chapter 9).

EXERCISE 14.5

Eating problem checklist

Do I or have I ever done any of the following?

- ⊙ deliberately missed meals or dieted extremely in other ways
- ⊙ eaten large amounts of food in a rushed, distressed state
- ⊙ taken laxatives because I feel I have eaten too much
- ⊙ made myself sick after eating
- ⊙ exercised obsessively in order to burn off calories
- ⊙ used speed, diuretics or slimming tablets to try and lose weight

Do you have any concerns about any of the above. If so write these down.

EXERCISE 14.6

If you have ticked any of the problems listed in Exercise 14.5, think about the pros and cons of what you do.

How does it help you? (See list at end of chapter.)

Is it successful?

Do you have any concerns? What are the problems? (See list at end of chapter.) Write these down.

Benefits of my eating pattern   Costs of my eating pattern

Then think about the pros and cons of change (see p. 58 for how to set this out).

(see p. 58 for how to set this out).

EXERCISE 14.7   **Test your knowledge!**

True or false?

1 The average woman needs 2,100 calories a day before doing any physical activity.
2 The female body should have about 25 per cent fat.
3 Eating fat is bad for you.
4 Muscle weighs more than fat.

5 Having any fat on your body means your are overweight and that's unhealthy.
6 What someone weighs is their personal responsibility. You have complete control over your weight and body shape.
7 Short-term fluctuations in weight are the result of the energy content of your last meal.
8 Chaotic eating, missing meals and extreme dieting reduce your metabolism which makes it harder for your body to lose weight and easier to gain weight.
9 Vomiting brings up most of what you have eaten.
10 Laxatives help you lose weight.

EXERCISE 14.8

Keep a diary of whenever you do any of those things listed above. What feelings trigger binge eating? (boredom/anger/loneliness/self-hatred)

What do you really want at these times?

⊙ someone to give you time and attention
⊙ to feel better about yourself
⊙ excitement . . . distraction
⊙ anything else?

Discuss this and see if you can plan alternatives (e.g. to bingeing on food, spending or shoplifting). Can you describe the cycle you go through with your eating (dieting, bingeing, dieting, etc.)?

What ideas do you have about how you could break that cycle?

E
X
E **14.9**   Solutions quiz
R
C
I   Here is a list of problems. See if you can find the solutions. See
S   end of chapter, but only after you have tried to work them out for
E   yourself!

1 People with eating problems end up believing the messages we
   are often given that being thin makes you happy. (If they are
   unhappy when they lose weight they may think this is because
   they haven't lost enough so have to lose more.) Or they think
   that other problems (e.g. lack of confidence) will be solved by
   losing weight.

   Possible solution:

2 People with eating problems usually think they are considerably
   bigger than they actually are. Most people who develop eating
   problems are actually normal weight. If people are overweight
   they often feel this is disastrous and that they can never be
   happy or successful at that weight.

   Possible solution:

3 Many people with eating problems fear that if they eat normally
   they will become grossly overweight, or if they don't carefully
   control what they eat they will lose control.

   Possible solution:

4 When people worry a lot about their weight they either weigh themselves frequently (once, twice, or more times a day) or can't bear to know what they weigh so avoid it altogether.

Possible solution:

5 Extreme dieting leads to hunger and a drop in blood sugar level, which leads to craving then over-eating. Rigid rules set you up to 'fail'.

Possible solution:

6 Research shows that people also binge when they have difficult emotional states – when they are bored, lonely, depressed or angry, people end up turning to food to block out these feelings or distract themselves.

Possible solution:

7 Foods consumed during a binge are nearly always forbidden foods which don't take any preparation (sweets, biscuits, cakes, etc.) and tend to be higher in calories. When people binge on these foods they think of them as dangerous high-risk foods so avoid eating them (but end up eating them whenever they binge).

Possible solution:

8 Most binge-eating is done in secret. Also, people with eating problems often feel ashamed so don't tell anyone about their problem.

Possible solution:

9 When people binge they eat very hurriedly, often standing up and putting one food after another in their mouth.

Possible solution:

10 When people binge they feel totally out of control. It seems like other people are able to control what they eat. The urge to binge seems to come over them very suddenly as if there is nothing they can do about it.

Possible solution:

11 They tell themselves that either they have to be totally in control (able to starve themselves), or they have to be totally out of control. When they eat 'forbidden food' they then don't stop until they have gorged themselves. People with bulimia think that they can't change their eating habits because if they eat forbidden foods they will lose control and binge more.

Possible solution:

12 People who diet excessively get so preoccupied with dieting that they count calories all the time and buy low-fat foods even when they are a healthy weight, or don't consume excess fat. People with eating problems think any fat in foods is bad for you.

Possible solution:

13 When you know you can vomit this gives you a freedom to eat everything you normally deny yourself.

Possible solution:

14 If you break your food rules you have to get rid of it.

Possible solution:

15 People with eating problems try to make one or two changes, but when things don't work out they give up and think what the hell!

Possible solution:

BODY IMAGE

If you have an eating problem, or hate yourself at times (see Chapter 11), then you are likely to have a negative body image. In Western cultures women are judged by their body size and learn to evaluate their self-worth by their body image more than by who they are as people or their achievements. Like all the problems we have addressed, learning to accept your body will not happen overnight, but it is something you can cultivate with patience and determination.

EXERCISE **14.10** 1 What is your body image at the moment? How do you see yourself/estimate your body size? How do you feel about your body/evaluate your image of your body?

2 What is the difference between your actual size and your body image? Why do you think you are discontented with your body image?

3 Learn to make friends with your body as it is naturally (i.e. the weight you are when you are not trying to change your natural body size). What will you need to do differently?

What do you avoid (looking at yourself, wearing certain clothes, etc.)?

What is your self-talk? (See chapter 7.)

Write a list of how you can make friends with your body.

4 Identify your negative self-talk and beliefs. Check these against the distorted thinking we discussed in Chapter 7.

How can you challenge these thought patterns and beliefs?

What thoughts, beliefs and self-talk do you need to have instead?

Write these down on a cue card and practise them night and morning for the next 14 days. (Remember you need to make affirmations realistic and believable.)

5 Treat yourself as if you care about and value yourself by eating well and taking regular exercise. Nurture and look after your body with moisturisers, aromatherapy baths, etc. This will help you to feel better about yourself and your body.

LAXATIVE ABUSE

If you misuse laxatives, consider your reasons for doing this. Do you believe they will help you lose weight? Are you doing it to give yourself an empty feeling? Why do you like that feeling? This may be about more than trying to lose weight. It may be that it neutralises bad feelings you carry inside, perhaps from things that were done to you that were not your fault. If you use laxatives in this way read Chapter 9 on child abuse or Chapter 11 on self-harm.

Laxative abuse is the most dangerous way of trying to feel thinner or reduce your weight. It is very important for your health that you try and come off them. If you don't you can cause irreversible damage to your lower intestine. Examine the pros and cons of this, as we have with other problems. Make a list of what you get from taking them, then think of all the drawbacks (e.g. the cost, the time spent in the loo, how that interferes with your life). Then write down the drawbacks about giving them up – constipation, rebound water retention (these should be short term), and the benefits (saving money, not having your life ruled by needing to go to the toilet). Discuss the problem with your doctor. He or she may suggest a safer alternative type of laxative.

GIVING UP LAXATIVES

If you decide to give them up and you haven't been taking them long (or in quantity), you can probably stop them all. Many people find they have to give them up gradually, either reducing how many they take or how often.

- If you gain weight don't panic. This is water and will correct itself in time. Try to avoid using diuretics instead as these can also become addictive. Cut out salt from your diet completely, and if necessary take a natural diuretic like vitamin C. If you have terrible water retention you will need to do this under the supervision of a dietician or your GP.
- Expect to feel bloated and more constipated at first. Eating regular meals and increasing the fibre in your diet (whole cereals, fresh fruit and veg and dried fruit) will help reduce constipation, but bran is not recommended. Drink plenty of water.
- Any reduction is progress. Well done. Don't be discouraged by setbacks and take one day at a time.
- Consider changing from a stimulant (such as Senakot) to a bulking laxative (such as milk of magnesia) which causes less damage to your gut.

HEARING VOICES AND SEEING THINGS THAT AREN'T THERE

If you hear voices this does not mean you are mad. Research shows that approximately 10 per cent of healthy people have had hallucinatory experiences at least once. Intrusive memories or hallucinations are also common when someone has been traumatised. Memories of traumatic experiences can be triggered, and it can seem as if they are happening now. This phenomenon was first identified in soldiers after the First World War and was called 'shell shock'. We call these 'flashbacks'. People who have been abused as children may hear the voice of the person who abused them or see their image. Often the image or voice is threatening them or telling them they are under their control. You may hear voices which tell you that you must or must not do things (e.g. that you must hurt yourself or someone else). If so, it is important for you to tell your GP or a mental health professional about this.

If this ever happens to you here are some things you can do to try and deal with it:

- Distract yourself by listening to music, a 'walkman', humming, or singing.
- Answer it back or shout at it. Shout 'go away'.
- Prove that it's not real, try to touch it.
- Use cue cards. Repeat phrases to yourself over and over, such as 'I can do this. This is old stuff; you don't rule me now. You can't hurt me any more.'

If the problem persists medication can be helpful and is worth trying.

APPENDIX

Risks of compulsive sex and intimacy

⊙ Pregnancy, wanted or unwanted. A brief relationship is not a good basis for having a baby. You will probably end up bringing the child up alone, which is very difficult. You may not have dealt with your own problems enough to be ready to start a family.
⊙ Sexually transmitted disease, including HIV but also STDs which can cause infertility.
⊙ Being thought easy game and used and abused, reinforcing our bad feelings about ourselves.
⊙ Feeling ashamed and worried about what others think about us.
⊙ Possible violence or other exploitation (e.g. prostitution, drugs).

Possible benefits of eating problem behaviours

⊙ It keep me focused on something which helps me forget my other problems.
⊙ It promises an answer to my problems and gives me something I can do to solve them.
⊙ It helps block out painful feelings or memories.
⊙ It helps me feel I am getting rid of something bad inside me.
⊙ It's a legitimate problem for which I can get other people to show me care and concern.

Possible costs to an eating problem

⊙ It affects my health (list how).
⊙ I hate bingeing – I feel out of control.
⊙ I don't enjoy making myself sick.
⊙ I'm fed up with it taking over my life.
⊙ It limits what I can do (e.g. I can't eat out with people).

True or false?

1 True. Those calories are need to keep you warm, pump your heart and maintain many other body functions.
2 True. 35 per cent of your diet should be fat.
3 False. You need fat on your body for various functions, to protect your organs, help keep you warm, etc.
4 True. If you exercise a lot and acquire more muscle your weight may go up.

5 False. Fat is there for protective reasons. For example, after the menopause larger women are healthier than slim women because the presence of fat protects their bones.
6 False. Your weight and body shape is also genetically and biologically determined. Most women are destined to be pear-shaped and have large hips for child-bearing.
7 False. Short-term weight change is the result of the fluid and weight of the food in your stomach, not its energy content.
8 True. Eating regular meals is a very important way of keeping your metabolism healthy. People who diet habitually have a sluggish metabolism.
9 False. When you vomit you will retain approximately 20 per cent of what you have eaten. This is one of a number of reasons why self-induced vomiting is not a good dieting strategy.
10 False. Laxatives reduce your weight because they take water from the bowel. However, this is not permanent weight loss from loss of fat – the calories in the food have already been digested in the small intestine.

Solutions quiz

1 Honestly evaluate whether your eating disorder 'works' for you? Find other ways of tackling problems.
2 Question and challenge the feelings that you are overweight if your weight is medically healthy. Find out what a medically healthy weight range is for someone of your height and compare this to what you would like to be.
3 Experiment with change. Test out your fears.
4 Try and find a middle way. Weigh yourself occasionally. If you want to weigh yourself regularly aim to do this no more than once a week. If you are doing it more often reduce this at a pace you can cope with.
5 You cannot overcome an eating disorder whilst trying to lose weight. You need to eat regular meals. By eating more regularly the urge to binge will reduce.
6 You need to identify which feelings trigger bingeing or purging and then find other ways of managing these feelings.
7 Try to give yourself permission to eat all the foods you enjoy and introduce these gradually into what you allow yourself.
8 Try not to be alone at risk times (e.g. visit someone after a meal, plan activities which will occupy or distract you). Consider telling people you trust about your problem. If you live with someone it may help to talk to them about how you feel after you have eaten. (It is helpful for them to understand that they cannot stop you purging and shouldn't try or criticise you or be disapproving when you do.)
9 Try and slow down a binge. Aim to always eat on a plate, put one food on your plate at a time and eat with a knife and fork. Try and leave the kitchen when you eat – you will be less likely to reach for something else.
10 and 11 Control isn't black or white. It's variable. One helpful strategy for some people is to practise delaying a binge by a minute, then two, then five

minutes. You will need to practise this regularly and build it up to learn that there are degrees of being in or out of control.

Similarly you can learn to have smaller binges. There are a number of things you can do to stop sooner. Prepare something to eat that you enjoy, like your favourite sandwich, rather than just eat instant food. If you binge on chocolate try cutting it up and eating one piece at a time. Plan to do something else whenever you binge, like go out or have a bath, and do this after eating less than when you usually binge.

12 Try and give up calorie counting. Fat is part of a normal diet. You shouldn't buy low fat foods unless you are medically overweight.

13 Make a firm commitment to yourself not to vomit. This is very likely to reduce how much you eat when you binge.

14 You need to change your food rules and the way you think when you eat things you have told yourself you shouldn't. Practise telling yourself things like 'I deserve this. It's OK to eat this. Other people allow themselves to eat these foods.'

15 You need to persevere. Things won't change overnight.

REFERENCES AND FURTHER READING

Butler, G. and Hope, T. (1995). *Manage your Mind: The Mental Fitness Guide*. Oxford: Oxford University Press.

Love and sex

Norwood, R. (1985). *Women Who Love Too Much*. UK: Arrow Books.
Orbach, S. and Eichenbaum, L. (1984). *What do Women Want?* UK: Fontana.

Eating problems

Buckroyd, J. (1989/1994). *Eating Your Heart Out: Understanding and Overcoming Eating Disorders*. London: Optima.
Cannon, J. and Einzig, H. (1983). *Dieting Makes You Fat*. London: Sphere Books.
Cash, T.F. (1997). *Body Image Workbook: An 8-step Program for Learning to Like Your Looks*. Oakland, Calif.: New Harbinger.
Kano, S. (1990). *Never Diet Again*. London: Thorsons.
Saunders, T. and Bazalgette, P. (1993). *You Don't Have to Diet*. London: Bantam.
Treasure, J. and Schmidt, U. (1993). *Getting Better Bit(e) by Bit(e)*. Hove: Psychology Press.

Review of Chapter 14

Please circle your answer to each of the following:

How much of the chapter did you read?

0%   25%   50%   75%   100%

Overall, was it

Very helpful   Helpful   Not relevant to me   Don't know   Unhelpful

Did you/your client complete Exercise 14.1?

Yes   No

Was it

Very helpful   Helpful   Don't know   Unhelpful

Did you/your client complete Exercise 14.2?

Yes   No

Was it

Very helpful   Helpful   Don't know   Unhelpful

Did you/your client complete Exercise 14.3?

Yes   No

Was it

Very helpful   Helpful   Don't know   Unhelpful

Did you/your client complete Exercise 14.4?

Yes   No

Was it

Very helpful   Helpful   Don't know   Unhelpful

Did you/your client complete Exercise 14.5?

Yes   No

Was it

Very helpful   Helpful   Don't know   Unhelpful

Did you/your client complete Exercise 14.6?

Yes   No

Was it

Very helpful   Helpful   Don't know   Unhelpful

Did you/your client complete Exercise 14.7?

Yes   No

Was it

Very helpful   Helpful   Don't know   Unhelpful

Did you/your client complete Exercise 14.8?

Yes   No

Was it

Very helpful   Helpful   Don't know   Unhelpful

Did you/your client complete Exercise 14.9?

Yes   No

Was it

Very helpful   Helpful   Don't know   Unhelpful

Did you/your client complete Exercise 14.10?

Yes   No

Was it

Very helpful   Helpful   Don't know   Unhelpful

Comments

What then?

After you stop chasing the highs or escaping from painful states, you may have to face a lot of feelings inside which will feel really uncomfortable. Hopefully the programme has helped you learn new coping mechanisms. But the painful negative feelings and beliefs you developed may take many years to heal. If you experienced abuse, neglect or major loss in your childhood, the pain will always be there but you can learn to tolerate it and be less overwhelmed. The first step is accepting the pain and making friends with it. Mindfulness practice (meditation), looking after yourself and living your life with care will help build positive states of mind. As you manage your problems more effectively, your relationships will improve and your life will get better. Gradually the happy times will increase and the bad times lessen. But you will always be vulnerable to setbacks. Also, part of your emotional roller-coastering is your temperament. This won't change much. (Look on the bright side. Life will never be dull!) Keep the manual and your notes and, whenever you need to, re-read them.

Each person will have different issues they will need to keep working at. Maybe you will continue to feel attracted to people who are unlikely to treat you well and feel that others you meet are unattractive or boring. Maybe you will continue to try to please people in the hope they will like you. Having supportive friends who understand your problems is very important. You need to remember to keep a middle way; that is, share your problems openly but not overburden people. This may not be easy for you. If your problems continue to be overwhelming and you still often feel suicidal, you may need continuing support from a CPN, psychologist or psychotherapist. The mental health service may also be able to offer you group work that will help you, such as assertiveness training or a psychotherapy group. If you have had substance abuse problems, AA or NA can be very helpful. There are meetings every day in big cities which are open to anyone.

Don't be discouraged by setbacks. They are inevitable, and dealing with them is part of how you will reinforce your new strengths. Problems like substance misuse, bulimia or self-harm may return at times of stress. At these times you need to go back to the manual and follow the steps again, remembering those which were most helpful to you. Go back to using the emotions diary (p. 66). This diary is very helpful for reflecting on your coping strategies and considering alternatives.

SAYING FAREWELL TO YOUR THERAPIST OR KEY WORKER

Hopefully you feel you have begun to trust those people providing your treatment and feel they've understood you a little. You may have developed quite strong attachment and feel upset at the thought of the sessions ending or never seeing them again. These feelings are very natural. You may want to control the ending by stopping the sessions early, so you feel less rejected or let down. It is important to talk about these feelings rather than act on old patterns (remember 'schema avoidance'!)

Try and keep a sense of what they have meant to you without needing to see them. This may not be easy for you. It may be appropriate for you to move on and let go of them, or it may be appropriate for you to have follow-up sessions to review your progress. If you end all contact (if you are moving away or decide this is the best thing to do), you could write to them. If so, it's helpful to agree that they won't need to respond.

WHAT NEXT?

The tasks for you in the next part of your personal journey in life will include:

- Forming and keeping healthy relationships. This will mean making friends in a way that isn't just based on you trying to please them. It could mean learning to like and not be bored by partners who are kind and stable, rather than bad to you but exciting.
- Developing a network of people who are trustworthy and supportive, not people who are likely to pull you back into old habits like taking drugs or drinking heavily.
- Developing a sense of who you are and a sense of purpose in life. This will mean making life goals; maybe learning something new, taking a course, pursuing something you are interested in. Having a spiritual faith may also be helpful for you and gives many people a meaning to their life.
- Learning to enjoy your own company and do things for yourself. Remember that feelings can follow actions. So take good care of yourself (a healthy diet, lifestyle, exercise) and your environment. This will help you to value yourself. Developing new skills will help you to feel more confident, whether this is taking adult literacy, learning to drive or learning how to do things for yourself at home.

John O'Donohue (1997) says that we need to find a spiritual home within ourselves:

The recovery of our soul . . . is vital in healing our disconnection . . . A time comes when you can no longer wallpaper this void. Until you really listen to the call of this void you will remain an inner fugitive, driven from refuge to refuge, always on the run with no place to call home . . . When you acknowledge the integrity of your solitude and settle into its mystery, your relationships with others take on a new warmth, adventure and wonder . . . It is very difficult to reach that quality of inner silence. You must make a space for it so that it may begin to work for you.

(O'Donohue, 1997)

E
X
E   **15.1**   **Reflection**
R
C   What is your personal journey now? Are you able to be patient
I   and cultivate the skills and qualities you need to develop peace
S   and contentment? If not, how can you develop that patience and
E   cultivate those qualities? Who can help you with this?

EXERCISE 15.2   **Life plan**

What are your personal goals for the next month, etc.? Think of
your goals in the different areas of your life. Try and fill in as
many of the boxes as possible.

	Diet	Relation-ships	Hobbies	Work	Lifestyle	Family
1 month						
2–6 months						
6–12 months						
1–2 years						
2–5 years						

REFERENCE

O'Donohue, J. (1997). *Spiritual Wisdom from the Celtic World*. New York: Bantam Press.

Review of Chapter 15

Please circle your answer to each of the following:

How much of the chapter did you read?

0%   25%   50%   75%   100%

Overall, was it

Very helpful   Helpful   Not relevant to me   Don't know   Unhelpful

Did you/your client complete Exercise 15.1?

Yes   No

Was it

Very helpful   Helpful   Don't know   Unhelpful

Did you/your client complete Exercise 15.2?

Yes   No

Was it

Very helpful   Helpful   Don't know   Unhelpful

Comments

If you would like to send the author your comments on the programme these would be greatly appreciated. (Please send via the publisher.) You could include your comments after each chapter and your overall view of the manual.

Overall:

What was most helpful?

What in the manual did you not find helpful?

What problems did you experience using the manual?

Were you able to overcome them?

What suggestions would you make to improve the manual?

What suggestions would you make to improve the programme?

Any other comments or suggestions?

Index